GO LEGAL YOURSELF!®

Know Your Business Legal Lifecycle®

Second Edition

Kelly Bagla, Esq.

WILEY

Published by John Wiley & Sons, Inc., Hoboken, New Jersey.
Published simultaneously in Canada.

For general information on our other products and services or for technical support, please contact our Customer Care Department within the United States at (800) 762-2974, outside the United States at (317) 572-3993, or fax (317) 572-4002.

Wiley publishes in a variety of print and electronic formats and by print-on-demand. Some material included with standard print versions of this book may not be included in e-books or in print-on-demand. If this book refers to media such as a CD or DVD that is not included in the version you purchased, you may download this material at http://booksupport.wiley.com. For more information about Wiley products, visit www.wiley.com.

Library of Congress Cataloging-in-Publication Data

Names: Bagla, Kelly, author.
Title: Go legal yourself! : know your business legal lifecycle / Kelly
  Bagla.
Description: 2nd edition. | Hoboken : Wiley, [2021] | Includes index.
Identifiers: LCCN 2020051119 (print) | LCCN 2020051120 (ebook) | ISBN
  9781119745549 (hardback) | ISBN 9781119745563 (adobe pdf) | ISBN
  9781119745556 (epub)
Subjects: LCSH: Small business—Law and legislation—United States.
Classification: LCC KF1659 .B34 2021 (print) | LCC KF1659 (ebook) | DDC
  658.1/20973—dc23
LC record available at https://lccn.loc.gov/2020051119
LC ebook record available at https://lccn.loc.gov/2020051120

Cover Design and Art By: Kate Brand Design

SKY10022869_120120

They say 2020 is the year of the woman. I dedicate this book to two women who have taught me that every year is the year of the woman.

My dedications go to my loving sister-in-law, Surinder Bagla, who taught me how to love the English language, and to my loving mother-in-law, Judy Calamungi, who taught me how to love the simple things in life.

Your love and support have forever changed my life!

Contents

Foreword

If this book existed when I started my entrepreneurial career over 40 years ago when I began importing the first sheepskin boots into America, it would have saved me a lot of trouble.

The common thing all entrepreneurs share is the attitude, "I won't do that until I need it."

Because the very nature of starting out on your own path implies you are limited in capital and all of your efforts are focused on product development, production, marketing, and deliveries, the last thing you want to do is spend money on legal fees, which can "wait until we need those services."

I can still hear the words of my long-time lawyer: "Brian, why do you always come to me when you are in trouble? Why don't you run things by me before you start out?"

Robert Ringer wrote a hugely successful book, *Winning through Intimidation*, about how he kept getting left out of the deals he orchestrated in the real estate business, and the one line that resonated with me to the core was that "a DETAIL will always come back to haunt you." I can't tell you how many times I had to "fix" a situation at great cost because, at the time, it didn't seem important to complete the legal documentation.

I still continue to get into new businesses and now the legal checklist is a standard part of getting organized, just as important as the product and marketing.

And this is where Kelly's book *Go Legal Yourself®* is such a great resource for every aspiring business builder. In addition to all the start-up issues, she gives you a glimpse of what you are going to need as you grow more successful.

From a legal and documentation standpoint, you can be ahead of the issues and not spend a fortune in remedying things you overlooked.

Best wishes on your journey.

Brian Smith
UGG Founder, and author of *The Birth of a Brand*, a roadmap for entrepreneurs

Preface

If you get a chance to read any basic literature about chess, the simplest definition you will find is that it is a game of strategy and tactics. The strategy consists of setting midterm positioning advantages, whereas tactics focus on immediate maneuvers during the game. I have always thought running a business is a lot like playing chess, so it is only fitting that my clients affectionally gave me the name "Queen of Business Law®." In chess, unless you are looking a few moves ahead, you are doomed to fall into your opponent's trap. With each turn, you need to anticipate the moves that your opponent can make and the various options that you have. Similarly, in business, if you know the road ahead, you can anticipate industry changes or alteration in customer behavior, which will allow you to always be on the cutting edge. You can then build your business to outlast your competition and you can make the right moves, whether that's making a better mouse trap, growing your business, or choosing the right distribution channels.

As a business owner, I have firsthand knowledge of how hard it is to start a business, let alone make money at it. As an attorney, I also have firsthand knowledge as to what can go wrong with starting a business.

- Are you running a business and confused about what you need to do in your business from a legal perspective?
- Are you confused by the seeming never-ending list of legal considerations?

These are all issues that I have found to be common for all entrepreneurs. There is one thing that every entrepreneur and business owner has in common — we know the pains and heartaches of running a business, and if we're lucky, we can eventually become successful. But wouldn't it be nice to know from the inception of your business how to run it successfully?

Go Legal Yourself®, Know Your Business Legal Lifecycle® 2nd Edition is a guide for entrepreneurs and business owners that explains the four phases of a Business Legal Lifecycle®. Just like all individuals, we have a lifecycle, whereby we're born, we grow up, experience life, and eventually pass on. Unfortunately, we're not born with a road map, which would help us avoid the painful parts of life. Businesses also have a lifecycle but understanding the Business Legal Lifecycle® is the trick to running a successful business by knowing exactly where you are in your business so you can easily move from one phase to another, be it from Startup to Growth or from Established to Exit.

My four-phased Business Legal Lifecycle® was developed to help business owners understand the legal aspects of their business. This knowledge is important because you don't know what you don't know, and that's when costly mistakes happen. Every step in the Business Legal Lifecycle® requires you to take different actions and adjust your way of thinking. Throughout your Business Legal Lifecycle®, you will encounter challenges and have to make decisions that could affect the success and outcome of your business.

Paying attention to all aspects of your business is important for every business owner to ensure that you are legally compliant. The traditional answer to the question of when you need to pay attention to the legal aspects of your business is **all the time**. That advice is not wrong; however, business owners are often so busy in doing the work in their business that they don't have the time to work on their business.

You don't know what you don't know, the law is complicated, so I developed the Business Legal Lifecycle®, which is practical and easy to understand. In this book, I will go through the four phases of a business and why you need to take such steps to legally protect each phase of your business.

Enjoy the book.

Kelly Bagla, Esq.

A fellow entrepreneur

Business Legal Lifecycle®

The Business Legal Lifecycle® is the progression of a business in phases over time and is most commonly divided into four stages, Startup, Growth, Established, and Exit. Because running a business is a lot like playing chess, I have assigned chess pieces to the individual phases.

The Pawn represents the first barrier of protection. They work hard and are sacrificed. The Startup phase represents the hard work put into starting a company and trying to keep it afloat.

The Rook represents the castle walls, which protect the King, Queen, Bishop, and Knight. The Growth phase represents innovation, as owners try to grow their business with unique confidential ideas and personnel.

The Knight represents the professional soldier whose job it is to protect those of rank. The Established phase represents your company as being stable and known to consumers as a recognized brand.

The King is the most important piece in the game. If your King is captured, you lose the game. The Exit phase is the most important phase in your Business Legal Lifecycle®, as this is the phase that sets you up for retirement or to start another venture. Without proper planning and money, you can't do either.

PAWN	ROOK	KNIGHT	KING

About the Author

Kelly Bagla, Esq., the Queen of Business Law®, is an award-winning corporate attorney who practices in San Diego, California. She is a bestselling author, inventor, and top woman entrepreneur. She has been nominated for Business Woman of the Year, and was selected Top Lawyer and Attorney of the Month. Winner of the Best of 2020 Oceanside Business Services award, Kelly was also named in the Top 20 Successful Businesswomen to Watch by *Insights Success Magazine* and the Top Transformational Women Leaders by *Industry Wired Magazine*. She is a speaker, TV personality, a judge on *Everyday Edisons*, an Emmy award-winning TV show, and also the host of a podcast show called Go Legal Yourself® (get the App – it's free).

Kelly's depth of experience ranges from managing domestic subsidiaries for a Fortune 500 biotech company, to advising domestic and international clients for one of the world's strongest global law firms, to partnering in a San Diego boutique law firm.

She has successfully founded Bagla Law Firm, APC, and is also the founder and CEO of GoLegalYourself.com, an online company that sells legal tools to savvy entrepreneurs.

Kelly has authored two books: *Go Legal Yourself® First Edition* and *Go Own Yourself: Unleash Your Greatness So You Can Own Your World*. Both books support and promote entrepreneurship.

Kelly has been interviewed by prestigious publications such as *Investor's Digest, Business View, California Business Journal, SDVoyager, LAVoyager*, and *StarCentral*, to name a few, for her achievement, innovation, and determination in helping entrepreneurs start successful businesses.

She is a monthly contributor to *Homeland Magazine* and *San Diego Veterans Magazine*, where she provides legal business advice to the veteran community. Kelly was chosen to write a full chapter in *The Growth Formula* by Kal Reece, "How Industry Leaders Overcome Fear, Debt & Financial Challenges."

Kelly's passion is to help entrepreneurs achieve their dreams and she lives by her own motto: **"Grab the world by the pearls, it's yours for the taking!"** – by Kelly Bagla, Esq.

She and her husband, Brent, live in San Diego with their four beautiful dogs.

Kelly@golegalyourself.com
5857 Owens Ave, Ste 300
Carlsbad, CA 92008
Mobile: 760-525-4540
Work: 760-784-9109

Introduction

Everything You Need to Know about Your Business Legal Lifecycle®

> A smart man makes a mistake, learns from it, and never makes that mistake again. But a wise man finds a smart man and learns from him how to avoid the mistake altogether.
>
> – Roy H. Williams

Whether you play chess or not, the parallels of chess and running a business are clearly evident:

- You learn to look ahead
- You learn the value of sacrifice
- You learn the value of preparation
- You learn to anticipate your competitors' moves
- You learn to think outside the box
- You learn to win

The game of chess is about winning; it's about protecting a prized piece and engaging in war with the opponent who wishes to defeat you. There are differing strategies for both offensive and defensive play, and the wise chess player will have experience with both. Running a business is much the same, protecting something of value, your company, and engaging in war with your competitors who wish to win. The only way a business owner can successfully navigate the many obstacles that face a business is knowing exactly which phase you are in at all times in your business.

Every business has a Business Legal Lifecycle®. As a business owner, this is probably the last thing on your mind, but my legal experience has repeatedly shown that business owners who pay attention to their Business Legal Lifecycle® are usually the successful ones.

From the moment you make the decision to set up your business, you are automatically starting your Business Legal Lifecycle®. By reading this book you will hopefully learn the four phases of the Business Legal Lifecycle® and how to better position yourself for success. Each phase has its own challenges and rewards and knowing that your business has:

- a Startup phase
- a Growth phase
- an Established phase, and
- an Exit phase

provides you with a road map as to where your business is at any given time. As your business grows and develops, so do your business goals, objectives, priorities, and strategies. Knowing exactly where you are in your business can be the fine line that makes or breaks your business.

Some businesses start fast, grow fast, and fail or succeed fast. Many businesses start slowly, then build fast, grow faster, buy other companies, or get sold and molded into larger organizations. But every business has its own Business Legal Lifecycle®.

This book is designed to help you determine where you are in your Business Legal Lifecycle®, how to handle the legalities of that phase, and how to move to the next stage. As a business attorney, I have helped many business owners like you move from one stage to the next, and with every stage come new risks and rewards. With every stage also come new legalities to face. This book addresses important questions that entrepreneurs and business owners alike ask every day, which can have huge impacts on the business if not implemented correctly. Educating yourself about your Business Legal Lifecycle® will position you as a better business owner and help you create a successful business.

I have always loved the game of chess. Since playing chess requires the same thinking and strategies as running a business, I decided to use the following pieces to represent the four phases of your Business Legal Lifecycle®, which will help you visualize where you are in your business:

Startup Phase:

- The Pawn represents the first barrier of protection. They work hard and are sacrificed. The Startup phase represents the hard work put into starting a company and trying to keep it afloat.

Growth Phase:

- The Rook represents the castle walls, which protect the King, Queen, Bishop, and Knight. The Growth phase represents innovation as owners try to grow their business with unique confidential ideas and personnel.

Established Phase:

- The Knight represents the professional soldier whose job it is to protect those of rank. The Established phase represents your company as being stable and known to consumers as a recognized brand.

Exit Phase:

- The King is the most important piece in the game. If your King is captured, you lose the game. The Exit phase is the most important phase in your Business Legal Lifecycle®, as this is the phase that sets you up for retirement or to start another venture. Without proper planning and money, you can't do either.

PART 1

Startup Phase

The critical ingredient is getting off your butt and doing something. It's as simple as that. A lot of people have ideas, but there are few who decide to do something about them now. Not tomorrow. Not next week. But today. The true entrepreneur is a doer, not a dreamer.

– Nolan Bushnell

The Pawn represents the first barrier of protection. They work hard and are sacrificed. The Startup phase represents the hard work put into starting a company and trying to keep it afloat.

CHAPTER 1

What Legal Entity Should I Be?

As a practicing business attorney for 18 years, I have heard it all when it comes to incorporating a business. Many think that incorporating their business will help them cut the federal tax bill or avoid paying state income taxes completely. First-time entrepreneurs often have misconceptions about incorporation, usually resulting from an optimistic desire for lower taxes or third-hand advice from a friend or a friend's accountant. When small business owners fall prey to some of these myths, the consequences can range from higher taxes to misunderstanding their personal liability. To gain a better understanding of these myths, it's important that you understand some of these misconceptions surrounding incorporation.

- **Incorporating can help with avoiding state taxes:**
  Those starting a business in California might be jealous of neighbors in Nevada who don't have to pay state income taxes. Many entrepreneurs believe that they can incorporate in a low tax or no tax state and their business is not required to pay any income taxes. It sounds like a great strategy but it does not work. When it comes to state taxes, it does not matter where the business is incorporated. What generally matters is where the owner operates the enterprise. Those living and running a business in California still need to pay state taxes on the income earned in California even if the company is incorporated in Nevada. Moreover, Nevada requires an annual filing of the list of officers and directors of the corporation and requires a business license. These fees can add up very quickly and outweigh the benefit of paying no state taxes.

- **Incorporating protects the owner from all personal liability:**
    Incorporating is a critical step for separating an owner from the business, but it does not absolve the owner of all personal responsibility. As the proprietor of a business, the owner can still be held personally liable for the business in several situations. If a business proprietor signs a contract in the owner's personal name, personally guarantees a loan, does not keep up with corporate compliance paperwork, or commits a crime, the owner will be personally liable.
- **It's better to wait until a product is ready for the marketplace:**
    Many small business owners prefer to avoid legal paperwork until they absolutely have to deal with it. Some believe there is no need to incorporate until they start selling a product or service. This line of thinking is wrong on two counts: First, liability issues related to a business can arise long before products hit the marketplace; for example, an employee, independent contractor, or vendor might sue the owner for related reasons. The second reason to incorporate early is related to an owner selling the company, as it's more desirable to treat the sale proceeds as long-term capital gains than ordinary income. The stock in your company must be held for more than one year.

Make no mistake, it is critical to form a corporation for entrepreneurial activities to minimize personal liability. In some cases, these business legal entities can lower taxes, but incorporating should never be considered an easy way to avoid taxes.

Before I explain which legal entities exist and which one would be a good fit for you, it's important to understand what exactly is a startup.

What Is a Startup?

Merriam-Webster's dictionary defines a startup as "the act or an instance of setting in operation or motion." This is not a helpful definition to the newly formed business. The reality is that there is no one definition any two entrepreneurs or business owners agree on. Most say a startup is determined by its age, growth, revenue, profitability, or stability. Neil Blumenthal, co-CEO of Warby Parker, defines a startup as "a company working to solve a problem where the solution is not obvious and success is not guaranteed." Another entrepreneur, Adora Cheung, CEO of Adora, stated: "A startup is a state of mind. It's when people join your company and are still making the explicit decision to forgo stability in exchange for the promise of tremendous growth and the excitement of making immediate impact." The Small Business Association sums up the word startup, "In the world of business, the word 'startup' goes beyond a company just getting off the ground. The term startup is also associated with a business that is typically technology oriented and has high growth potential. Startups have some unique struggles, especially in regard to financing. That's because investors are looking for the highest potential return on investment, while balancing the associated risks."

The best definition of a startup was provided by Alyson Shontell while she was the editor-in-chief of *Business Insider US*. "A startup is an emotional roller coaster that can either result in massive failure or success, after which one's bank account total may either drastically increase or decrease. The person behind a startup is a founder, an often very bright, somewhat crazy person who finds a normal 9-to-5 job dull and is deluded into believing he or she can change the world by working tirelessly in front of a computer screen. The relentless work has been known to shave a few years off a founder's life while adding premature gray hairs, but it can be very rewarding both emotionally and financially for those who pursue it." I could not agree more with Alyson Shontell's definition.

Now that we have a definition of what a startup is, I can answer the number one most frequently asked question in the Startup phase.

What Legal Entity Should I Be?

When starting out, it is important to determine what form of business structure will work best for your specific situation. Choosing the best legal structure for your business requires knowledge of your line of work and understanding of local state and federal laws. The legal structure you choose for your business is one of the most important decisions you will make in your startup process. Your choice of structure can greatly affect the way you run your business, impacting everything from liability and taxes to control over the company. Choosing the right business entity allows an entrepreneur to reduce liability exposure, minimize taxes, and ensure that the business can be financed and run efficiently. It also provides business owners with a mechanism for ensuring that the business operations will continue, rather than be automatically terminated, upon the death of an owner.

When choosing a business entity, you should consider the following:

- Are your personal assets at risk from liabilities arising from your business?
- Are you able to offer ownership to key personnel?
- What are the continued costs of operating and maintaining your business?

Here is a list of the most commonly used legal structures for business and the advantages and disadvantages of each one is explained in detail below.

Common Legal Entities:
- Sole Proprietorship
- Partnership
- Limited Liability Company – including: Series LLC
- Corporation – including:
  - C Corporation
  - S Corporation
  - Close Corporation
  - Benefit Corporation
  - Professional Corporation
  - Nonprofit Corporation

Sole Proprietorship

The most common and simplest form of business is a sole proprietorship. Many small business owners launch their companies as sole proprietorships, in which they and their business are essentially one and the same. An individual proprietor owns and manages the business and is responsible for all business transactions, including its debt. If you want to be your own boss and run a business from home without a physical storefront, a sole proprietorship allows you to be in complete control. Sole proprietorships do have some advantages. They are quick and easy to set up, as no paperwork is required to be filed with the state, they do not require large amounts of money, and accounting is relatively simple. However, sole proprietorships have many disadvantages as well.

The biggest disadvantage is that there is no separation between the assets of the business and the owner's personal assets. This means that anyone who sues the business for any reason can potentially receive a judgment for the business owner's personal assets, such as cash kept in personal checking or savings accounts, the family car, or even the business owner's home. Another big disadvantage occurs if the sole proprietorship wants to borrow money. Because there is no separation between business and personal assets, many sole proprietors have to use their personal assets, such as their home, as collateral for a loan. If the business fails and the owner does not have enough money to pay off the loan, the lender can take the owner's home and sell it to get its money back. Needless to say, this type of ownership is the riskiest and, to make things worse, the courts do not see any difference between a sole proprietorship and its owner. So, when the owner passes away, the business ends.

Partnership

Other forms of business ownership include forming a partnership. This entity is owned by two or more individuals. There are two types of partnerships: a general partnership, where all is shared equally including the assets, profits, liabilities, and management responsibilities between the partners; and a limited partnership, where only one partner has control of the operations while the other partner contributes to and receives part of the profits. A partnership is ideal for anyone who wants to go into business with a family member, friend, or business partner. This entity allows the partners to share profits and losses and make decisions together. Having a well-drafted partnership agreement by an attorney is advisable so all the partners can be held responsible for their contributions, or lack thereof.

While general partnerships provide a means of raising capital more quickly and allow several people to combine resources and expertise, several problems commonly occur, such as partners having different visions or goals for the business, an unequal commitment in terms of time and finances, and personal disputes. Some advantages of a general partnership are shared financial commitment, the ability to pool resources, and generally, limited startup costs. Some disadvantages of a general partnership include partners being personally liable for business debts and liabilities, and each partner may also be liable for debts incurred by decisions made and actions taken by the other partners.

Limited Liability Company

A limited liability company (LLC) is a unique business entity that allows the owners to limit their personal liability while enjoying the tax and flexibility benefits of a partnership. Under an LLC, the members (owners) are protected from personal liability for the debts of the business, as long as it cannot be proved that the members have acted in an illegal, unethical, or irresponsible manner in carrying out the activities of the business.

Limited liability companies were created to provide business owners with the liability protection that corporations enjoy while allowing earnings and losses to pass through to the owners as income on their personal tax returns, thus avoiding double taxation (which is covered in the corporation section below). LLCs can have one or more members and profits and losses do not have to be divided equally among the members. There is a state filing required to form an LLC and although not required by law, drafting an operating agreement is highly advised as it is a crucial document. The operating agreement customizes the terms of the LLC according to the specific needs of its owners, along with outlining the financial and functional decision-making among the members. Businesses that do not have a signed operating agreement fall under the default rules outlined by the individual states, which can sometimes work against the wishes of the owners. In such a case, the rules imposed by the state will be very general in nature and may not be right for every business. For example, in the absence of an operating agreement, some states may stipulate that all profits in an LLC are shared equally by each member regardless of each member's capital contribution. This may not be fair to the members who have contributed a lot more money as opposed to the members who only contributed a fraction of the money.

Many states do not offer this next structure but it's worth mentioning as it is part of an LLC structure – a Series LLC. A Series LLC is a unique form of a limited liability company in which the articles of formation specifically allow for unlimited segregation of membership interests, assets, and operations into independent series. Each series operates like a separate entity with a unique name, bank account, and separate books and records. A Series LLC may have different members and managers in each series. The rights and obligations of these members and managers differ from series to series. Each series may enter into contracts, sue or be sued, and hold title to real and personal property.

The most important characteristic of a Series LLC is the liability protection that is available to each series. Assets owned by one series are shielded from the risk of liability of other series within the same Series LLC. A Series LLC is similar in concept to a corporation with several subsidiaries. However, the Series LLC concept is designed to segregate risk within separate entities without the cost of setting up new entities. The Series LLC is a creation of the individual states and only in certain states are Series LLCs allowed to be formed. Delaware was the first state to enact legislation authorizing the creation of Series LLCs. Several states and one territory have followed suit, including Illinois, Iowa, Nevada, Oklahoma, Tennessee, Texas, Utah, and Puerto Rico. Some states, like California, do not allow the Series LLCs to be formed under state law but Series LLCs formed in other states can register with the state of California and do business in California.

Corporation

The law regards a corporation as a legal entity that is separate and distinct from its owners. Corporations enjoy most of the rights and responsibilities that an individual possesses; that is, a corporation has the right to enter into contracts, loan and borrow money, sue and be sued, own and sell property, hire employees, own assets and pay taxes, and sell the rights of ownership in the form of stocks.

Corporations are used throughout the world to operate all kinds of businesses. While their exact legal status varies somewhat from jurisdiction to jurisdiction, the most important aspect of a corporation is the limited liability protection. This means that shareholders have the right to participate in profits but are not held personally liable for the company's debts.

There are several different types of corporations, including "C" Corporations, "S" Corporations, Close Corporations, Benefit Corporations, Professional Corporations, and Nonprofit Corporations. There are many differences between them and an understanding of each is required to decide which one is right for you.

C Corporation

A C Corporation is a business term that is used to distinguish this type of entity from others, as its profits are taxed separately from its owners under subchapter C of the Internal Revenue Code. This is known as "double taxation," whereby the C Corporation is taxed on its earnings or profits and the shareholders are taxed again on the dividends they receive from those earnings. A C Corporation is owned by shareholders, who must elect a board of directors who make business decisions and oversee policies. Because a corporation is treated as an independent entity, a C Corporation does not cease to exist when its owners or shareholders change or die. Some of the major benefits of a C Corporation include:

- Its owners (known as shareholders or stockholders) enjoy limited liability and they are generally not personally liable for the debts incurred by the corporation. They cannot be sued individually for corporate wrongdoings.
- It can deduct the cost of benefits as a business expense; for example, it can write off the entire costs of health plans established for employees.
- The corporate profits can be split among the shareholders and the corporation. This can result in overall tax savings, as the tax rate for a corporation is usually less than that for an individual.
- It can have an unlimited number of shareholders, as this allows the corporation to sell shares to a large number of investors, and allows for more funds to be raised.
- It allows for foreign nationals to have a right to own or invest in a C Corporation, which allows for diverse investors to participate in the business.
- It can offer different "classes" of stock, such as common or preferred, to different shareholders, which can help attract different groups of investors.

S Corporation

An S Corporation stands for "subchapter S corporation," a special tax status granted by the Internal Revenue Code that allows corporations to pass their corporate income, credits, and deductions through to their shareholders. Generally speaking, S Corporations do not pay income taxes as the company's individual shareholders divide the income among each other and report it on their own personal income tax returns. An S Corporation status lets businesses avoid double taxation, which is what happens when a business is taxed at both the corporation level and business owner level, such as with a C Corporation. An S Corporation must adhere to the following limitations:

- It must be a domestic corporation, which is based and operated in the United States of America.
- It can only have "allowable" shareholders, meaning that none of the shareholders can be partnerships, other corporations, or non-U.S. citizens.
- It cannot have more than 100 shareholders in total.
- It can only have one class of stock: common.
- All of the company's shareholders must unanimously consent to an S Corporation status.

An S Corporation offers several advantages, such as:

- It is exempt from federal income tax except for certain capital gains and passive income. It allows profits to pass through to its shareholders and the income is then taxed on the shareholder's personal tax returns at each shareholder's individual tax rates.
- It allows for limited liability protection for personal assets that are separate from the assets of the business. Shareholders are not personally liable for the company's debts or liabilities, and for the most part, creditors are not able to go after the shareholders personally to recover business debts.
- It allows for flexibility in how to characterize the income for tax purposes. As a shareholder of a corporation, you can also be an employee of the business and pay yourself a salary, which is taxed at your tax rate. In addition to your salary, you can pay yourself dividends from the corporation that are generally taxed at a lower rate than the employee salary. This helps reduce self-employment tax liability, as long as you are characterizing your salary and dividend in a reasonable way.
- It allows for easy transfer of ownership without causing significant tax consequences or terminating the corporate entity.

Close Corporation

A Close Corporation, also known as a family corporation, is generally a smaller corporation that elects close corporation status and is therefore entitled to operate without the strict formalities normally required in the operation of standard corporations. Many small business owners find this benefit invaluable. In essence, a Close Corporation is a corporation whose shareholders and directors are entitled to operate much like a partnership. The Close Corporation election is made at the state level and the state laws vary with respect to the eligibility of close corporation status and with respect to the rules governing them. Some states do not authorize them. The requirements to be eligible for a Close Corporation status include: no more than 30 to 35 shareholders, it cannot make a public offering of its stock, and shareholders must agree unanimously to a close corporation status. Close Corporations enjoy relaxed rules with respect to the formalities of governance, such as shareholders typically need not hold formal annual meetings and the shareholders may override the directors and act on their own.

Benefit Corporation

A Benefit Corporation is a relatively new type of business entity. Originally implemented by legislation in Maryland in 2010, this new entity is now recognized in half the states, while legislation is pending in many others. A Benefit Corporation is a for-profit corporation entity that in addition to profit also takes society and the environment into consideration when making decisions. The goal of this corporate structure is to encourage for-profit companies to identify social missions and demonstrate corporate sustainability efforts. To be recognized as a Benefit Corporation the company must include:

- Purpose: Benefit Corporations commit to creating public benefit and sustainable value in addition to generating profit. This sustainability is an integral part of their value proposition.
- Accountability: Benefit Corporations are committed to considering the company's impact on society and the environment in order to create long term sustainable value for all shareholders.
- Transparency: Benefit Corporations are required to report to their shareholders, and in most cases the wider public, in most states annually and using a third-party standard, showing their progress toward achieving social and environmental impact.

Becoming a Benefit Corporation has advantages for everyone in and related to your business, from shareholders and directors to your customers. These benefits include:

- Expanded Shareholder Rights: Investing in a Benefit Corporation gives impact investors the assurance they need that they will be able to hold a company accountable to its mission in the future. This could aid companies in attracting impact investment capital.

- Reputation for Leadership: Your business will join other high profile, highly respected companies as Benefit Corporations and be at the forefront of a growing movement.
- Attracting Talent: According to *Inc. Magazine* writer Peter Economy, by 2020, Millennials (those born between about 1980 and 2000) are forecast to represent half of the American workforce, and by 2025, 75% of the global workforce. Benefit Corporation status gives prospective employees confidence that a company is committed to their mission.
- Increased Access to Private Investment Capital: Benefit Corporation status can make your company more attractive to investors as a company with increased legal protection, accountability, and transparency around its mission. Benefit Corporations can also speed up investor due diligence, since they produce an annual benefit report, which describes their qualitative activities aimed at producing general public benefit.

Professional Corporation

A Professional Corporation, also known as "APC" or "PC" was created to allow certain kinds of professionals such as lawyers, doctors, accountants, and engineers to do business as a Professional Corporation. In each state, specific types of professionals are allowed, and in some states required, to form a Professional Corporation. For example, in California, professionals are required to form a Professional Corporation and therefore cannot be an LLC. Professional Corporations are different from the C or S Corporations because all shareholders in a Professional Corporation must be members of the same profession involved in the same business. For example, a group of lawyers can form a Professional Corporation if their business is to practice law. While there is some limitation on liability surrounding the actions of each partner, the professionals in the firm may not be relieved of liability of their own professional negligence or malpractice. This is the main reason professionals form this type of corporation. They can enjoy sharing management responsibilities and profits without exposing themselves to malpractice actions against the other owners.

Nonprofit Corporation

A Nonprofit Corporation is an organization whose purpose is something other than making a profit. A Nonprofit Corporation donates its revenue to achieve a specific goal that benefits the public instead of distributing it to shareholders. Being a nonprofit does not mean the organization will not make a profit. Nonprofits can make money but all of the money must go back to the organization by paying employee salaries, administrative expenses, and other overhead costs. No one person or group owns a nonprofit. While anyone can incorporate as a nonprofit, only those who pass the stringent standards set forth by the government can achieve tax exempt status.

Nonprofit Corporations are established for a specific noncommercial purpose, which usually includes churches, schools and universities, hospitals, museums, and shelters. There are four main types of nonprofits and each contains the ability to achieve tax exempt status despite their slightly different goals and corporate structure. They include:

- Public Charities: Typically, a charity provides low cost or free services to the public using funds received from the public. Funds can be obtained through private donations or fundraising events.
- Social Advocacy Organizations: This type of group is member based and sets out to achieve specific goals without achieving a profit. Funds are generated through member dues.
- Foundations: This type of organization works to better the community, whether contributing financially or as local charities holding events to benefit residents. Funds usually come from for-profit companies.
- Trade and Professional Organizations: People in the same organization can benefit from the activities of this type of nonprofit. Funds are primarily obtained through membership dues.

What Factors Should I Consider Before Choosing a Business Structure?

When deciding to set up a new entity for your startup, you should consider your startup's financial needs, risk, and the ability to grow. Here are some factors to consider when choosing the legal structure for your business, and always consult with your accountant, as these structures have very different tax implications:

- **Complexity:** How complex is your business and what entity best addresses your needs? When it comes to startup and operational complexity, nothing is simpler than a Sole Proprietorship. You simply register your company name, start doing business, report the profits, and pay taxes. However, you are personally liable for all debts of your company and it can be very difficult to procure outside funding in case you need money to purchase equipment or grow your business. Partnerships, however, require a signed agreement to define the roles and percentages of profits, but partners are still personally liable for the partnership debts. Corporations and LLCs have various reporting requirements with state and federal governments, but they offer limited liability protection for the shareholders and members.

- **Liability:** Is the entity you are forming protecting your personal assets from your business assets? A Corporation carries the least amount of personal liability since the law holds that it is its own entity. This means, generally, creditors can sue the Corporation but they cannot sue you personally to obtain access to your personal assets. An LLC offers the same limited liability protection but with the tax benefits of a Sole Proprietorship. If the business tax is lower than your personal tax bracket, forming an LLC is not always the best option. However, in some situations, an LLC may elect to be taxed as a Corporation. Partnerships share the liability between the partners as defined by their partnership agreement.

- **Flexibility:** Where is your company headed and which type of legal structure allows for the growth you envision? It is recommended that before you start your business, you should invest some time drafting a business plan. The benefits of a business plan are discussed at length in Chapter 7. Turn to your business plan to review your goals and see which structure best aligns with those objectives. Your entity should support the possibility for growth and change.

- **Taxes:** Will this entity provide the best tax benefits for your business? An owner of an LLC pays taxes just as a sole proprietor, whereby all the profit is considered personal income and taxed accordingly at the end of the year, unless you elect to be taxed as a corporation. As a small business owner, you want to avoid double taxation in the early stages and an LLC structure prevents that along with an S Corporation. Individuals in a partnership also claim their share of profits as personal income. Both C Corporations and and S Corporations file their own tax returns each year, paying taxes on profits after expenses, including payroll.

- **Control:** Who will have control over your business, and how do you maintain the majority control? If you want sole or primary control of the business and its activities, a Sole Proprietorship or an LLC might be the best choice; however, you are opening yourself up to personal liability. A Corporation has a board of directors that makes the major decisions that guide the company. It also has shareholders who have voting power. A single person can control a corporation, especially at its inception, by being the majority shareholder, but control of a company is shared with the board of directors.

- **Capital Investment:** Will you need outside investment money to start and run your business? If you need to obtain outside funding, such as from an investor, venture capitalist, or a bank, you may be better off establishing a Corporation. Corporations have an easier time obtaining outside funding than a Sole Proprietorship. Corporations can sell shares of stock and secure additional funding for growth, while sole proprietors can only obtain funds through their personal accounts using their personal credit or taking on partners.

- **Licenses, Permits and Regulations:** Will the licenses and permits be held in the name of your business? In addition to legally registering your business entity, you may need specific licenses and permits to operate. Depending on the type of business and its activities, it may need to be licensed at the local, state, and federal levels.
- **Changing a Sole Proprietorship:** Changing a Sole Proprietorship or a General or Limited Partnership to a Corporation or a Limited Liability Company can offer a range of advantages. Most notable is asset protection: An S or C Corporation or an LLC protects the owner's personal assets in case debts or legal judgments are claimed against the business.

What Are Some Advantages of Incorporating?

Owning a small business can be a risky venture. One way to limit your personal liability is by incorporating your business. While incorporation requires more paperwork and expense than a Sole Proprietorship or a Partnership, it offers important legal and tax advantages. Either way, incorporating is a good decision for most businesses, and despite popular belief, it is not just reserved for those that are wealthy businesses and well established. There are multiple benefits of incorporating, all of which you should fully understand before you decide to make your move.

Some of the most popular reasons why incorporating your business should be a priority are:

- **Protect your personal assets from creditors:** There is no doubt that starting your business is exciting, but with that excitement comes the reality that accidents happen and unfortunately businesses sometimes fail. This is where one of the best benefits of incorporating comes into play. By incorporating your business, albeit as a C or S Corporation, or an LLC, you are protecting your personal assets from business debts. If your business falls on hard times, your personal property is off limits to collection agencies. For example, if you cannot pay your business loan any longer, generally, the bank will not be able to come after your home to satisfy the loan. If you have not yet incorporated your business, your personal assets are linked automatically to your business. This may include your car, your home, your investment accounts, and even assets you obtain in the future. Additionally, if you were to file bankruptcy within your business, your personal assets would be used to repay your debt. By incorporating you protect your business from this, which is probably one of the most valuable benefits of incorporation.

- **Protecting your personal assets from lawsuits:** Along with the protection from creditors comes protection from lawsuits filed against your business. Without incorporating, your personal assets remain at risk to anyone filing a lawsuit against your business. These individuals could try to collect on a judgment against you, for example, by taking possession of your home. That means if a customer trips and slips in your store and takes you to court to collect damages, you are personally liable. Incorporating, however, creates a solid barrier between your personal assets and the claims of others. That means if your business is sued, the safety of your personal and family possessions is not at risk. As a responsible businessperson you never want to be caught unprepared. The benefits of incorporating lead specifically to keeping your business operational and the security of yourself and your family intact.
- **Tax benefits and money savings:** Another benefit of incorporating your business, and one of the most crucial to leverage, is the many tax deductions that are available to incorporated businesses. When you go from being a Sole Proprietor or Partnership to a business structure such as an LLC or an S or C Corporation, there are numerous deductions at your disposal that are not available to individuals. Everything from tax deductions on health insurance and life insurance, to saving on self-employment taxes. Side bar: Tax laws are complex, and it is in your best interest to consult with an accountant before claiming any deductions.
- **Easier to raise capital:** It might not be the most obvious benefit of incorporating, but it is true that by incorporating you are making it easier for your business to raise capital. This mostly means that if you plan on borrowing money or applying for a loan, it adds a sense of legitimacy to your business. If you want to accept money from outside investors, you simply sell stock of your company and if you want to borrow from banks, the lenders are more likely to loan you money because your business assets can be held as collateral.
- **Easier to sell:** Corporations and LLCs are generally much easier to sell and are usually more attractive to buyers than a Sole Proprietorship. This is mainly because a new buyer will want to limit their legal and tax exposure and not be personally liable for any wrongdoing on the part of the Sole Proprietorship. If someone buys a Sole Proprietorship, the new owner can be held personally liable for any mistakes or illegalities on the part of the prior

owner, even if the new owner had nothing to do with those activities. This is usually not the case with a Corporation or a Limited Liability Company.

- **Protect your brand:** Another benefit of incorporating your business has to do with your brand. Your brand is more than a logo or a marketing phrase. It is the way you operate your business, the look and feel of your location, and the type of products or services you offer. When you incorporate your business, it is not just your name you are protecting; you are also protecting the business overall image. You have worked hard to build your brand and image. By incorporating you can protect it from being used by others for their benefit.

- **Perpetual existence:** When you incorporate, you create a separate and distinct legal entity. This separate and distinct entity can exist almost forever, irrespective of what happens to the shareholders, directors, or officers. It is important to know your business can still be sold or that you may close it at some point. However, with the definition of a Corporation is the business's ability to remain in perpetual existence as its own entity. This important benefit matters because it gives you the ability to create a long-term plan for growth within the business. Investors want to know that your business can go on without you, legally, and it allows the business to remain operational without the need to reestablish itself. That being said, perpetual existence becomes a powerful and necessary tool for any business that wants to establish a strong foundation from which to grow. Corporations have unlimited life.

- **Transfer your business more easily:** Here's one of the benefits of incorporating that many people often miss. Let's say that you want to pass your business on to your child as you get older, but only want to do so in the event of a sudden illness. It is easier to transfer ownership when your business is a Corporation than it is if you are running a Sole Proprietorship. Remember, in a Sole Proprietorship, all of your personal assets are linked to your business. It is not possible to easily value your business for a sale or transfer it to another person until each of these lines of connections to your personal assets are defined and cut. Whether for short- or long-term goals, your business will benefit significantly from incorporating for this reason alone. There are some restrictions, of course, but transferring funds and even business ownership is easier when the business has its own identity.

- **Privacy and confidentiality:** Perhaps the most important benefit of incorporating for some people is the level of privacy that comes with incorporating your business. When you incorporate, you can keep your personal identity hidden. All of your business affairs are private and kept confidential unless you choose to disclose them. Some states do not even require your name to be on any business documents at all.

- **Increases credibility:** Both customers and venders feel more secure and confident dealing with an incorporated entity, be it a Corporation or an LLC as opposed to a Sole Proprietorship. Most businesses that are not incorporated actually miss out on gaining business from the bigger companies due to the fact that the giants of industry simply do not want to deal with individuals. If disputes occur, the giants do not want to be publicly viewed as the bully taking a small individual to court. Therefore, they just do not give their business to Sole Proprietorships. Having an "Inc." or an "LLC" after your company's name adds credibility and a touch of professionalism to your business dealings, and has the possibility to attract more business.

While it may not be necessary for all businesses to incorporate, most of the time, businesses do benefit from going through the incorporating process. It may seem like a daunting task at first, but with the help of GoLeglYourself .com tools, the process of incorporating is made easy.

If I Incorporate, Are My Personal Assets Protected from Lawsuits?

Once your company is incorporated, the limited liability protection afforded by the incorporation process is NOT automatic, meaning once you incorporate your business, your personal assets are not automatically protected from lawsuits. Ninety percent of business owners think they can enjoy the limited liability protection afforded to them by their incorporated entity. Incorporated entities do not automatically become barriers between your personal assets and your business assets whereby your personal assets are protected from lawsuits. The company actually must comply with corporate formalities in order to enjoy that limited liability protection for your personal assets. The protection afforded by incorporated entities is limited in nature because a Corporation is a separate entity and the law requires the business owner to treat it as such.

There are certain corporate compliance steps you must take in order for you and your company to enjoy limited liability protection under the law. Corporate compliance includes you treating your incorporated entity as completely separate from yourself. In most cases, you may only be one person running the company, but the law requires you to treat the company as if it is a completely separate entity from you. Moreover, failure to file required paperwork can lead to fines and penalties, including suspension of your incorporated entity.

The corporate compliance paperwork is key to keeping your company in good standing with the state where your company is incorporated. If your business is sued, the person suing may try to show the court that you have not maintained your business to the letter of the law, thus "piercing the corporate veil" and attaching your personal assets as part of a judgment. Piercing the corporate veil refers to a circumstance in which courts set aside limited liability protection and hold a company's owner personally liable for the organization's activities or debts. While the laws vary from state to state, courts will generally abstain from piercing the corporate veil unless there have been signs of serious misconduct.

Below is a general overview of what you should to do to keep your business in compliance with the law. Of course, specific requirements will vary based on your business type and location:

1. **File an annual report:** Most states require some sort of annual report filing on the anniversary of your incorporation date.
2. **File amendments for any changes:** If you make major changes to your corporation, you may need to keep your state up to date with filing Articles of Amendment. Examples of change include changes to the company name, changes to the registered agent, changes to the business address, an increase in the number of authorized shares, and changes in business activities.
3. **Keep up to date with any meeting minutes:** If your business is a Corporation, you'll need to record meeting minutes whenever you hold a corporate meeting. The bare minimum requirement regarding meeting minutes are the annual minutes, which appoint directors and officers.
4. **File a DBA for any name variations:** A lot of times, a business has an official name and then uses any number of variants of that name or in some cases uses different names to do business. In these cases, you should file a DBA (Doing Business As) with the county where you do business for each name used.
5. **Get an EIN:** You must obtain a Federal Tax Identification number, also known as an Employer Identification Number (EIN). An EIN is a unique nine-digit number that is as important for your company as a social security number is important for you personally. An EIN is used to open a bank account, register your company with various agencies, and file company taxes, and is required by clients who pay for your products or services.
6. **Separate bank accounts:** You will need to open a separate bank account for your incorporated entity that has its own checks and its own credit cards. This action separates your personal money from your business

money and prevents any commingling. Having a separate business account will make it easier for you to manage your business and show separation from personal assets, thus proof of a separate entity existence for your business. Additionally, this action will allow your incorporated entity to start creating its own credit rather than using your personal credit.

7. **Use full legal name:** The name of the corporation should be used in full, including "Inc." or "LLC," on all contracts, invoices, and documents used by your company. This clearly indicates the existence of the incorporated entity as a separate entity.

8. **Use your title:** Always use your title, such as President, Chief Executive Officer, or Secretary, when signing on behalf of your incorporated entity, as using the name of the corporation and your title further creates separation from you as an individual. Furthermore, if you were going to get sued, generally, by using your title, the person or entity suing you can only sue you as a corporate officer and not you as an individual person.

Key Takeaways

- When starting out, it is important to determine what form of business structure will work best for your specific situation. Choosing the best legal structure for your business requires knowledge of your line of work and understanding of local, state, and federal laws. The legal structure you choose for your business is one of the most important decisions you will make in your startup process. Your choice of structure can greatly affect the way you run your business, impacting everything from liability and taxes to control over the company.

- When deciding to set up a new entity for your startup, you should consider your startup's financial needs, risk, and the ability to grow. Take into consideration these factors when choosing the legal structure for your business and always consult with your accountant, as these structures have very different tax implications.

- Once your company is incorporated, the limited liability protection afforded by the incorporation process is NOT automatic, meaning once you incorporate your business, your personal assets are not automatically protected from lawsuits. Ninety percent of business owners think they can now enjoy the limited liability protection afforded to them by their incorporated entity. Incorporated entities do not automatically become barriers between your personal assets and your business assets whereby your personal assets are protected from lawsuits.

CHAPTER 2

What Other Documents Do I Need?

Starting a business can be overwhelming, and not knowing what you need is even worse. Filing a name for your entity with the state can be the easy part; running your business like a business is the hard part. I am frequently contacted by business owners who have just filed their name with a state and don't know what other documents are required for their startup. The incorporation process requires more than the initial filing of the Articles of Incorporation, also referred to Certificate of Incorporation or Articles of Organization, which are a set of formal documents filed with a government body to legally document the creation of an incorporated entity.

As mentioned in the previous chapter, the law regards a corporation as a legal entity that is separate and distinct from its owners. Corporations have the right to enter into contracts, loan and borrow money, sue and be sued, own and sell property, hire employees, own assets and pay taxes, and sell the rights of ownership in the form of stocks. The only way to treat your corporation as a legal entity that is separate and distinct from you as an individual is to have a number of legal documents that make up the internal governing rules of your business, creating the separate and distinct function.

The following documents are required of an incorporated entity, which show the separate existence of the entity and further solidify the need for limited liability protection:

- **For a Corporation – Bylaws:** Bylaws are a detailed set of rules adopted by the corporation's board of directors after the company has been incorporated. They are an important legal document, capturing procedures affecting the governance of the corporation. Generally, the bylaws set forth the responsibilities of the directors and officers, the manner of calling meetings of the shareholders and directors, the maintenance of corporate records, the issuance of reports to shareholders, voting and proxy procedures, and general corporate matters. The following requirements must be included in your bylaws:

- Name, purpose, and location of your company
- Voting rights and selection of the shareholders
- Maximum and minimum number of directors allowed on the board
- Duties and responsibilities of shareholders, directors, and officers
- Time, place, and location of meetings, including the type of meeting
- Specific rules for amending any current bylaws
- **For an LLC – Operating Agreement:** An operating agreement is a key document used by LLCs, as it outlines the company's financial and functional decisions including rules, regulations, and provisions. The purpose of the document is to govern the internal operations of the business in a way that suits the specific needs of the business owner. Once the document is signed by the members of the limited liability company, it acts as an official contract binding them to its terms. Here are some reasons why you would need an operating agreement:
  - It provides member protection from personal liability, as without this document your LLC can closely resemble a Sole Proprietorship and jeopardize your personal liability.
  - If members have orally agreed to certain terms, misunderstanding or miscommunication can take place. It is always best to have the operational conditions and other business arrangements handled in writing so they can be referred to in the event of any conflict.
  - State default rules govern LLCs without an official operating agreement. The state default rules are so general, it is not advisable to rely on a governing state to manage your agreement.
- **Sole Incorporator Resolution:** The incorporator is the person who signs the Articles of Incorporation. This person could be you or someone else. Once the Articles of Incorporation are filed with the state, the incorporator will sign the Sole Incorporator Resolution appointing the board of directors and will generally resign as the sole incorporator as to avoid any further liability.
- **Organizational Meeting Minutes:** Organizational meeting minutes are the minutes of the first shareholder meeting to approve and agree on all the actions of the incorporator. The organizational meeting minutes will appoint officers, reaffirm the directors, issue shares, approve bylaws, and allow for the setting up of bank accounts.
- **Founder's Stock Purchase Agreement:** A founder is the person who founded the company. A founder's stock purchase agreement allows the

founders to document their initial ownership in the company, including standard transfer restrictions and any vesting provisions with respect to their shares.

- **Subscription Agreement:** A Subscription Agreement is an agreement between the company and the investor that sets out the price and terms of the purchase of shares in the company. The subscription agreement details the rights and obligations associated with the share purchase and provides evidence of such ownership in the company.

Now that you know what initial documents are required as part of the incorporation process, what other documents are needed to actually conduct business? The second question most frequently asked in the Startup phase relates to what other documents are needed.

What Other Documents Do I Need?

Unless you are a contract law attorney, you probably don't lie awake at night asking yourself, what is a contract? Is my contract protecting me? But in our modern economy, we live in a world that is, in many ways, defined by contracts. We wake up in our home that was purchased with a real estate sales agreement. But before we purchased, the builder entered into contracts with the seller of the land, subcontractors, the real estate agent, construction material suppliers, and probably a bank for financing. Then we get into our car for which we entered into a purchase agreement or sales contract. The car dealer perhaps has a commercial lease for the dealership building and numerous agreements with one or more car manufacturers. We arrive at work, and many of us walk into an office environment in which we can look around and see evidence of dozens of contracts – office lease, supplies, furniture, internet providers, telecommunications, and utilities, just to name a few. All of these providers probably have hundreds or thousands of contracts.

Many people think of all these business and contractual relationships as a relatively recent phenomenon. This couldn't be further from the truth. While it is true that the complexity and number of contracts have increased, contracts have been around for centuries, from Ancient Egypt to Medieval Knights. In fact, they are the reason commerce is possible today. If we look at the history of contracts, business started with bartering, the face-to-face hand-off of goods, which was the earliest and simplest form of a contract. Then came the oral contracts, which made more complex commerce possible by bringing the promise of future delivery into play, all based on the traditional handshake, which ensured a form of a contractual promise. And finally, the written contracts, which marked the shift from handshake to tangible contracts.

Contracts are legally binding agreements and are involved in almost every aspect of your business life. Contracts are essential for business dealings because they are binding on all parties. If one party doesn't hold up its end of the bargain, the other party has legal remedies for damages. A contract serves as a guide to the agreement that must be followed by both parties. It presents each party with the opportunity to:

- Describe all obligations they are expected to fulfill
- Describe all obligations they expect the other party to fulfill
- Limit any liabilities
- Set parameters, such as time frame, in which the terms of the contract will be met
- Establish payment terms
- Establish all the risks and responsibilities of the parties

All businesses will need contracts and what types of contracts you'll need will vary depending on the nature of your business and where you are in your Business Legal Lifecycle®. However, common contracts that most businesses in the Startup phase require, and should have, include a promissory note, client contract, employment contract, and independent contractor agreement. These contracts are discussed in further detail below.

- **Promissory Note:** One of the greatest concerns for any startup is money. Where do you get money to start your company, and where do you get money to keep your company going? The four most common sources of startup capital are:
  1. Personal savings
  2. Family and friends
  3. Cash flow from the business
  4. Credit cards

  When using personal savings or money from family and friends, some startups treat this money as a loan that the startup intends to pay off over time. A promissory note is a financial instrument that contains a written promise by one party to pay another party a definite sum of money, either on demand or at a specified future date. A promissory note typically contains all the terms pertaining to the indebtedness, such as the principal amount, interest rate, maturity date, date and place of issuance, and the signatures of the parties involved. If you make a loan to your startup, the promissory note provides evidence of indebtedness, which once your startup makes a profit, you can repay yourself without paying taxes on that sum of money. Without a promissory note, it will be hard to convince an Internal Revenue agent that you made a loan to your company and that sum of money should not be accounted as part of the company profits. It also shows that you are treating your company as a separate entity and not as your personal piggy bank, which could cost you your limited liability protection.

- **Client Contract**: A good client contract does not have to be complicated. Its goal is to establish all the expectations of a project and working relationship up front. We all understand the importance of contracts, but that does not mean we always use them, or use the right ones. For years, you may have skated by without taking a client contract seriously, or maybe you hastily downloaded one from the internet. Maybe you immediately sign whatever document a client sends your way, or maybe you don't have any kind of contract at all. A client contract is not intended to create traps with legal fine print, but rather to make sure everyone is on the same page when it comes to important details like project scope, deliverables, payment timeline, and other contingencies.

  At its core, a good client contract should spell out who's doing what, when, and for how much. Keep in mind that clunky legal terms just confuse people. I went to law school and my eyes still glaze over whenever a client contract is full of legalese. As a standard rule of thumb, don't include anything in a client contract if you don't know what it means. Here are some important areas you'll need to include in your client contract:

  - **Contact Information**: Every client contract should include the full legal business name, main contact, and physical address for both the client and you.
  - **Project Details:** Be as specific as possible as to what you are being hired to do. For example, if you are being hired to redesign a website, are you responsible for the new copy? Will the client provide the copy? Does the scope of the project include other aspects like search engine optimization? The goal is to set expectations and guide the working relationship with some predefined parameters.
  - **Payment Terms**: These are the most important terms of your client contract so be very specific as to how you are being paid. Are you going to be paid on an hourly basis or by the project? If it's hourly, you may want to stipulate a minimum or maximum hour range to avoid surprises. If you get paid by the project, be sure to lay out the exact deliverables. In addition, you should spell out how quickly the client needs to pay upon receiving an invoice and what are the acceptable payment methods.
  - **Schedule:** Be extremely clear about any deadlines, including final deliverables as well as any project milestones, and definitely include that any client delays could or may hinder the schedule.

- **Termination:** You should agree with the client on what the terms of termination of your project will be. To ensure you are paid for your time, state that any received payments are non-refundable should the project be terminated without cause. Usually, termination occurs once the project is complete and you are paid in full. However, due to extenuating circumstances, the project may have to be terminated early. At all times, your client contract should stipulate what will happen upon termination of the agreement, which allows for your compensation for the work already completed.
- **Working Relationship:** Due to laws being very strict when it comes to employment law, and companies can get into a lot of trouble with tax agencies for incorrectly categorizing employees as contractors, your client contract should define the working relationship by adding some language that states that you are being hired as an independent contractor and will be responsible for paying your own taxes.
- **Choice of Law:** In the U.S., contracts can actually specify where disputes will be handled and which state's laws will govern those disputes, with some exceptions. This might be helpful if you and your client are located in different states. Unless you have a particular reason for picking another state, for example, some large corporations choose to be governed by the state of Delaware, which can be more favorable to business, you would choose your own state to govern your disputes. After all, it can be costly and time consuming to travel out of state to defend and settle a dispute.
- **Arbitration Clause:** You may want to include an arbitration clause in the client contract. If any disputes arise related to the contract, a neutral third party will hear the evidence and make a decision. The benefit of arbitration is that it's typically faster, simpler, and easier to schedule than courtroom litigation. In addition, arbitration is a private matter and will not become public information, which gives the parties involved some privacy.
- **Employment Contract:** Employment contracts are vital for legally defining the relationship between your business and your employee. For example, an employment contract will create a strong basis for protecting both your company's interests and the employee's specific role in the company. An employment contract should be created for each new employee and tailored toward their specific role. Some of the important details that should be covered in an employment contract would include:
- Details of the position offered
- Primary duties and responsibilities that the role includes
- Details of salary and other compensation
- Duration of employment, whether it be permanent or for a fixed period of time

- Details of any benefits such as holiday entitlement, pension, bonuses, and health insurance plans
- Restrictive covenants or a non-compete stating the employee cannot work for a competitor or start a competing business within a specified time frame and location
- Reasons and grounds for termination
- How and where to handle disputes
- Confidentiality guidelines

The need for an employment contract cannot be stressed enough. Here are three major reasons why they are a must-have for any business:

1. **Confidentiality:** Many job positions give employees access to confidential company information and data. An employment agreement will contain a confidentiality clause that protects the company's intellectual property from employees divulging sensitive information to others. A non-compete clause usually goes hand in hand with the confidentiality clause. A non-compete prevents the employee from working for any competitors for a certain period after the employment ends. This provides the company with extra protection for their confidential information.

2. **Reduced Risk:** Ensuring both parties (employer and employee) are in agreement as to the terms and conditions of the employment reduces the risk of confusion. The employment agreement becomes binding and serves to reduce the chance that one party will have grounds for legal action later down the road.

3. **Setting Expectations:** Stating exactly what you expect from an employee in their role, standards of performance, and what is deemed acceptable and unacceptable behavior should be spelled out clearly. Communicating this to the employee from the outset will reduce the amount of time you spend speaking with them, advising them, and correcting their behaviors.

- **Independent Contractor Agreement:** Hiring an independent contractor to work for you sounds like it should be easy. There's no complex paperwork the way there is with an employee – you just shake hands and get going, right? Not quite. With laws now imposing more restrictions with hiring independent contractors, an independent contractor agreement will be one of the most important contracts your business will use. An independent contractor is a worker who is not legally considered an employee of a company. Independent contractors, also called freelancers or consultants, are usually self-employed and provide products or services to their clients for payment.

When hiring an independent contractor, a company is not responsible for withholding any taxes from the worker's paycheck. For example, companies hiring employees must withhold taxes and pay Social Security and Medicare taxes, and pay unemployment tax on wages. This is not the case when you hire an independent contractor. Companies are not required to withhold taxes from the worker's paycheck or provide any sick pay, maternity leave, or other similar benefits. Here are some details that must be addressed in an independent contractor agreement:

- Details about the services or products being purchased by the company
- The terms and duration of the services or products being offered
- Payment terms of when and how the independent contractor will be paid
- Confidentiality clause
- Dispute resolution clause

You should be aware of the legal differences between an independent contractor and an employee. This is the area where most companies will get themselves in a lot of trouble with tax authorities and usually end up paying vast amounts of money in penalties, fines, and fees. Here are some big legal and logistic differences between an independent contractor and an employee:

- Independent contractors are self-employed
- Independent contractors work for more than one company
- Independent contractors send invoices to their clients
- Independent contractors hire their own employees or contractors to help them with projects
- Independent contractors control where they work
- Independent contractors control exactly how work is completed
- Independent contractors use their own equipment to complete projects

Each state has its own definition of what is considered an independent contractor and it is advisable to check with your local business attorney before hiring an independent contractor. In addition to the above list and state-specific definitions, the Internal Revenue Service has its own checklist of 20 factors that define an independent contractor. This checklist is based on common law as developed in past court cases and administrative hearings. For your reference, this 20-factor checklist is provided on the website. Furthermore, the Employment Development Department (EDD) has its own list of employment classification when it comes to labeling someone an independent contractor. Provided for your reference is the checklist from the EDD.

Each state has its own laws pertaining to business contracts and contract law and depending on where you incorporate your business, that state's law will generally govern the contracts you use. It is always advisable that you consult with a business attorney in your area to make sure you are entering into the right contracts with the right people.

How Do I Protect My Business from Lawsuits?

Starting and running your own business can be incredibly rewarding but it's also inherently risky. Maybe you're doing something entirely new and putting your money, time, and dreams on the line to make it a success. Rest assured, you are not alone. Many entrepreneurs take the same path to follow their dreams of success, but sometimes things don't go as planned, and getting sued, for example, could destroy everything you've worked so hard to build. So what are your chances of getting sued? What can you do further to protect your business?

The threat of a lawsuit is very real as there are millions of cases filed in U.S. state courts every year. To assess your chances of being sued, the first step is to figure out where you could potentially be liable or otherwise legally and financially responsible. Contract disputes are a very common source of liability for businesses and tort cases are another risk area. This type of lawsuit includes slip and fall cases, employment discrimination, and even wrongful death suits.

Of course, not everyone has the same type of level of risk. Your chances of getting involved in a lawsuit can depend heavily on your exposure. For example, if you have a business storefront, it's possible that you could get sued by someone who slips and falls on your property. In contrast, if your business only operates online, you don't have the same exposure. Having employees is another risk factor, as well as signing a large number of contracts, especially if they are complex. It's possible that even your own success may expose you to lawsuits as competitors could file claims to slow your progress or disgruntled employees could make claims that aren't valid. Valid or not, lawsuits are not cheap.

Although there's always some risk that goes along with being a business owner, the threat of a lawsuit should not discourage you from living your dream. Below are simple ways to protect yourself and mitigate some of the potential damage of lawsuits:

- **Well-Drafted Contracts:** Contracts are critical to any business, and having a well-drafted legal contract may save your business a lot of money if an issue arises. Even if you do everything right, there is still a chance your business will be confronted with a lawsuit at some point. Here are some clauses that should be included in your contract to help mitigate damages:

- Alternate dispute resolution, such as mediation or arbitration, should be included in your contract, which can be a viable way to resolve issues while avoiding the costs of trial, provided both sides agree.
- A force majeure clause can excuse a party's non-performance that results from unforeseen and uncontrollable events. For example, if you were unable to deliver an order of goods to your client due to your products being destroyed by extreme weather conditions, having this clause in your contract could prevent your client from suing you, since the delay was caused by something that was out of your control. Without this clause, your client would have grounds to sue you for breaching the contract.
- An attorneys' fees clause can be helpful to prevent litigation, as it ensures that a prevailing party in any lawsuit may be able to recover their attorneys' fees and costs from the non-prevailing party. This will cause either party to think twice before filing a lawsuit, since the costs of losing can be very high.

- **Keep Good Records:** In a fast-moving world of handshakes and oral contracts, not everyone takes the time to enshrine day-to-day deals in writing; however, there's nothing like having well-documented facts on your side to prove your argument or to avoid conflict all together. Keep notes on discussions and meetings and anything else that could help your case.
- **Obtain Reputable Business Insurance:** Purchasing business insurance is an investment in your company that protects your long-term financial health. For an added layer of protection, it is always advised and is good practice for your business to retain general liability insurance from a reputable insurance company. Once you have incorporated, your second order of business should be to determine your specific insurance needs based on the nature of your business. No business owner can foresee every issue that might impact operations, which is why it's crucial to find the insurance policies that are best suited to your business. The types of policies you need are determined by your business operations, its location, exposure to risk, and a variety of other factors. Here is a list of some of the more common insurance policies business owners buy:
  - **General Liability Insurance:** Most businesses need general liability, one of the most common policies. General liability provides coverage for customer injuries and damage to customer property at your business.
  - **Errors and Omissions Insurance:** An errors and omission (E&O) policy is designed to protect you and your employees from claims by clients or customers of inadequate work or negligence. While this protection

might not be required in your industry, it's advisable for any business that provides services to a client.

- **Workers' Compensation Insurance:** Workers' compensation coverage provides benefits to an employee who becomes injured or ill on the job. It also protects business owners from liability. Regardless of the level of risk associated with your business, workers' compensation is required in most states for businesses with employees.

- **Product Liability Insurance:** If your business sells products to the general public, product liability insurance is a must. Product liability policies work to protect a business in a case where harm could be caused by your products or if your business is named in a lawsuit due to damage.

- **Vehicle Insurance:** If company vehicles are used in your business, those vehicles should be fully insured to protect your business against liability if an accident should occur.

- **Business Interruption Insurance:** If a disaster or catastrophic event does occur, the operations of a business will likely be interrupted. During this time, your business will suffer from lost income due to your staff's inability to work in the office, manufacture products, or make sales calls. This type of insurance is especially applicable to companies that require a physical location to do business, such as retail stores. Business interruption insurance compensates a business for its lost income during these events.

While shopping for insurance, you will want answers to several key questions, such as:

- What risks must be covered?
- How much coverage will be sufficient?
- What are the deductibles?
- Are the coverage limits high enough?
- What items or occurrences are excluded from coverage?
- Are there any gaps in my coverage?

By having the right insurance in place, a business can avoid a major financial loss due to a lawsuit or catastrophic event. There are many different types of insurance policies that may apply to your particular situation, so before you buy insurance, understand which one or ones are right for you.

Key Takeaways

- All businesses will need contracts and what types of contracts you'll need will vary depending on the nature of your business and where you are in your Business Legal Lifecycle®. However, common contracts that most businesses in the Startup phase require and should have include a promissory note, client contract, employment contract, and independent contractor agreement.

- The threat of a lawsuit is very real as there are millions of cases filed in U.S. state courts every year. To assess your chances of being sued, the first step is to figure out where you could potentially be liable or otherwise legally and financially responsible. Contract disputes are a very common source of liability for businesses and tort cases are another risk area. This type of lawsuit includes slip and fall cases, employment discrimination, and even wrongful death suits.

- Although there's always some risk that goes along with being a business owner, the threat of a lawsuit should not discourage you from living your dream. Knowing some of the simple ways to protect yourself and mitigate some of the potential damage of lawsuits could limit your exposure.

CHAPTER 3

How Do I Protect My Brand?

Branding is a way of identifying your business; it's how your customers recognize your products or services. A strong brand is more than just a logo; it's reflected in everything from your customer service style, to your business cards, to your marketing materials. Your brand should reflect what your business stands for and what sets it apart from your competitors. It expresses the qualities, strengths, and personality of your business. Branding should be considered in the early stages of your startup, as launching a business with a strong brand could give you a greater chance of success.

Everyone's idea of branding is different. Some people think it's simply the fonts and colors a company decided to use. But if you've got a real understanding of what a brand is, you know that it includes at least some of the following:

- Design (logo, colors, font)
- Marketing
- Taglines and slogans
- Look and feel

As the world's richest man, Jeff Bezos, states: "A brand is literally what people say about your business when you're not in the room."

What Are the Benefits of Branding?

The main objective of branding is to establish a significant and a distinguished presence in the market and the industry as a whole that attracts loyal customers and retains them. Some benefits of branding your business are:

- **Standout:** If you are a small business or creative entrepreneur, you may have realized that there are a lot of us. A good brand has a clear purpose and will help you stand out among your competitors. First impression is everything.
- **Credibility:** When a business has solid branding, it increases that company's credibility within its industry, as well as with customers. Having an established and clear brand will provide you with the appearance of an expert.
- **Customer Loyalty:** Good branding elevates a business and builds recognition and loyalty. Once customers begin to recognize and buy a service or product, a good brand can keep them coming back for more, and can make loyal buyers of that brand.
- **Client Retention:** People connect with brands that share the same values. If your brand clearly represents your business, you'll be more likely to attract the right people. For example, if you have a high-end jewelry store and you want to attract a higher-paying client, your branding needs to be in line with high-end quality jewelry.
- **New Product Introduction:** If you already have loyal customers and a strong brand, it will be easier to introduce new products or services. Your audience will already be interested in what you sell, so they will be more inclined to buy new products you are offering.

What Are the Different Types of Branding?

There are many types of branding strategies that have worked well over the years for many of my clients, but the important question for you is – which type of branding is right for your business? The type of brand you choose can help guide your business decisions and should be incorporated into your overall business planning. Keep in mind that different types of brands suit different products and services and will appeal to different customers. Some top brand strategies include:

- **Corporate Branding:** The overall company must have its own brand of trustworthiness, quality, and usefulness that people acknowledge as such. Corporate branding refers to the practice of promoting the brand name of a corporate entity, as opposed to specific products or services. Usually, the public will associate the corporate brand with what the company stands for, the quality of products or services it offers, and its overall personality. Examples of some well-known corporate brands are: Coca-Cola, McDonald's, Apple, Disney, and Google, to name a few.
- **Personal Branding:** Just as the name suggests, personal branding refers to branding for individuals as opposed to branding for a whole business. Your

personal brand is how you promote yourself. It is the unique combination of skills, experience, and personality that you want the world to see. Personal branding is used to differentiate yourself from other people. Examples of some well-known personal brands are Donald Trump, Richard Branson, Oprah Winfrey, Tony Robbins, and Elon Musk, to name a few.

- **Product Branding:** This is the most common and easiest type of branding. Product branding is a symbol or design that identifies and differentiates a product from other products. Have you noticed how "Kleenex" has become a word synonymous with "tissues"? That's because the product has reached the pinnacle of product branding success, the type of branding that gets customers to choose one product over another based on the brand alone. Examples of some product branding at its best are Colgate used for toothpaste, Windex used for window cleaner, Coca-Cola used for soft drinks, Tylenol used for pain relief, and Pledge used for furniture polish.

As you consider the different types of branding that have made many companies successful, think about the type of branding you want for your company and how it can help you become noticed and eventually successful.

Now that you know a little more about branding, we can proceed to the third most frequently asked question in the Startup phase.

How Do I Protect My Brand?

As previously mentioned, a brand is a name, term, design, or symbol that distinguishes your products or services from other products and services so that it can be easily recognized, communicated, and marketed effectively. We're all familiar with the concept of tangible property. It's a possession or something you own that you can touch and feel. However, there is also a class of property for things that are considered intellectual property, such as works of art, music, designs, inventions, and your company name and logo. This intellectual property can be protected by patents, trademarks, trade secrets, and copyrights. Your brand becomes your company's intellectual property that potentially creates value over time.

One of the biggest parts of a brand is the company name and logo. Talking to clients over the years about their business name and logo, I found that they are initially not too concerned about protecting them from the outset. Their reasoning is simple: they think that since they are using the name and logo, no one else can use it. This could not be further from the truth. Under common law, if you choose not to protect your business name or logo through some sort of formal registration with the United States Patent and Trademark Office

(USPTO), then you have a common law right to use them. If, however, a third party files for registration protection with the USPTO for the same name or logo used by you, under the first to apply rule, more than likely the third party will be granted the right to use your company name and logo. At that time, you will be legally required to cease and desist using the very name you may have created a business under and the logo you spent a lot of money on designing and securing.

Here are a number of ways you can protect your brand:

- **Patent:** A patent is a right granted to an inventor by the USPTO that permits the inventor to exclude others from making, selling, or using the invention for a period of time. The patent system is designed to encourage inventions that are unique and useful to society. There are three different kinds of patents:

  1. **Utility Patent:** The most common type of patent is a utility patent, which protects the way an invention functions and how it is used. If you have a new, useful invention that is not obvious to others in the field of the invention, you might qualify for a utility patent. Utility patents are grouped into five categories: a process, a machine, a manufacture, a composition of matter, or an improvement of an existing idea. If you acquire a utility patent, you can stop others from making, using, selling, and importing the invention. This prohibition is valuable, as it allows you to develop an exclusive market to sell your invention. A utility patent lasts for 20 years from the date that the patent application is filed.

  2. **Design Patent:** If you create a new and original design that ornaments a manufactured device, you may qualify for a design patent. A design patent is granted for product designs, for example, an IKEA chair or a Manolo Blahnik shoe. The design patent must be ornamental or aesthetic, it cannot be functional. Once you acquire a design patent, you can stop others from making, using, selling, and importing the design. You can enforce your design patent for only 14 years after it is issued.

  3. **Plant Patent:** The least frequently issued type of patent is the plant patent, which is granted for any novel, nonobvious, asexually reproducible plant. Unless you are a research scientist or agricultural expert, it is somewhat unlikely that you will apply for a plant patent. A plant patent lasts for 20 years from the date that the patent application is filed.

For an invention to qualify for a patent, it must be both novel and nonobvious. An invention is novel if it is different from other similar inventions in one or more of its parts. It also must not have been publicly used, sold, or patented by another inventor within a year of the date the patent application was filed. An invention is nonobvious if someone who is skilled in the field of the invention would consider the invention an unexpected or surprising development.

Here is a list of things that are patentable:

- Computer software and hardware
- Chemical formulas and processes
- Drugs
- Medical devices
- Furniture design
- Jewelry
- Fabrics and fabric design
- Musical instruments

A patent cannot be obtained for a mere idea or suggestion. Here is a list of things that are not patentable:

- Abstract principles
- Fundamental truths
- Calculation methods
- Mathematical formulas

If your intellectual property qualifies to apply for patent protection, you must apply with the USPTO within 1 year of publicly disclosing the invention. Usually, you or your patent attorney would conduct a preliminary patent search before applying for a patent to determine if it is feasible to proceed with the application. The application and the fee are submitted to the USPTO where it is reviewed by a patent examiner. If a patent is granted, the inventor must pay another fee and the USPTO publishes a description of the invention and its use. After a patent expires, the invention becomes public property and can be used or sold by anyone.

- **Trademark:** The USPTO defines a trademark as "a word, phrase, symbol, or design, or a combination of words, phrases, symbols, or designs that identifies and distinguishes the source of the goods of one party from those of others." A trademark not only gives the trademark owner the exclusive right to use the mark but also allows the owner to prevent others from using a similar mark that can be confusing for the general public. Here are some of the top reasons why trademarking could be important to your business:
  1. **Value:** There are few business assets that not only create immediate value, but grow in value. The more your business expands and improves, so

does the value of your brand. Customers associate trademarks with every part of your business and confusing it with another company can be fatal for you. One of the biggest advantages of having a registered trademark is that a valid trademark can be bought, sold, licensed, and used as a security interest for acquiring a business loan. If a startup hopes to expand, sell, merge, or raise funding, a registered trademark is a must.

2. **Expanding:** The biggest problem in waiting to apply for a national trademark is having your name and logo limited to a small geographic area. A startup could have local protection where they operate, but find out later a national trademark prevents them from expanding. Consider trademarks not just for today but in future plans to expand into new areas.

3. **Save Money:** Trademarking your name and logo from the start could save you thousands down the road, as a complete search would be conducted before you spend the money creating a business name that is already owned by another. Many small businesses are unaware of potential problems until they receive a strongly worded demand letter from a company on the other side of the country threatening legal action if they do not change their business name immediately. The letter may ask for thousands in damages, not to mention the thousands you'll pay to rebrand your company.

4. **Perpetuity:** Other intellectual property protections like patents have a shelf life. Drug companies get years to sell their pharmaceuticals before other companies can sell cheaper generics. Trademarks will last for eternity, as long as you file an occasional renewal form. As far as business investments go, nothing lasts longer and provides more long-term opportunities than a trademark.

5. **Protection:** Trademarking is an important step for protecting your brand identity. It will stop competitors from poaching your customers by imitating your brand. As a registered trademark owner, you can bring suit in federal court for trademark infringement and prohibit others from using your mark.

In order to qualify as a registered trademark, a mark must be distinctive; that is, the mark must be capable of identifying the source of a particular good. In determining whether a mark is distinctive, the courts group marks into four categories, based on the relationship between the mark and the underlying products: arbitrary or fanciful, suggestive, descriptive, or generic. Because the marks in each of these categories vary with respect to their distinctiveness, the requirements for, and degree of, legal protection afforded a particular trademark will depend upon which category it falls within.

- **Arbitrary or Fanciful Mark:** This is a mark that bears no logical relationship to the underlying product. For example, the words "Exxon," "Kodak," and "Apple" bear no inherent relationship to their underlying products (respectively, gasoline, cameras, and computers). Similarly, the Nike "swoosh" bears no inherent relationship to athletic shoes. Arbitrary or fanciful marks are inherently distinctive, capable of identifying an underlying product, and are given a high degree of protection.
- **Suggestive Mark:** This is a mark that evokes or suggests a characteristic of the underlying good. For example, the word "Coppertone" is suggestive of suntan lotion, but does not specifically describe the underlying product. Some exercise of imagination is needed to associate the word with the underlying product. At the same time, however, the word is not totally unrelated to the underlying product. Like arbitrary or fanciful marks, suggestive marks are inherently distinctive and are given a high degree of protection.
- **Descriptive Mark:** This a mark that directly describes, rather than suggests, a characteristic or quality of the underlying product, such as its color, odor, function, dimensions, or ingredients. For example, "Holiday Inn," "All Bran," and "Vision Center" all describe some aspect of the underlying product or service (respectively, hotel rooms, breakfast cereal, optical services). They tell us something about the product. Unlike arbitrary or suggestive marks, descriptive marks are not inherently distinctive and are protected only if they have acquired "secondary meaning." Descriptive marks must clear this additional hurdle because they are terms that are useful for describing the underlying product, and giving a particular company the exclusive right to use the term could confer an unfair advantage. A descriptive mark acquires secondary meaning when the consuming public primarily associates that mark with a particular company rather than the underlying product. Thus, for example, the term "Holiday Inn" has acquired secondary meaning because the consuming public associates that term with a particular provider of hotel services, and not with hotel services in general. The public need not be able to identify the specific company, only that the product or service comes from a single company. When trying to determine whether a given term has acquired secondary meaning, courts will often look to the following factors: (i) the amount and manner of advertising, (ii) the volume of sales, (iii) the length and manner of the term's use, and (iv) results of consumer surveys.
- **Generic Mark:** This a mark that describes the general category to which the underlying product belongs. For example, the term "Computer" is a generic term for computer equipment. Generic marks are entitled to no protection under trademark law. Thus, a company selling "Computer" brand computers, such as Apple, would have no exclusive right to use that term

with respect to that product. Generic terms are not protected by trademark law because they are simply too useful for identifying a particular product. Giving a single company control over use of the term would give that company too great a competitive advantage. Under some circumstances, terms that are not originally generic can become generic over time and thus become unprotected.

Although most companies generally use a (TM) sign for claiming their right to their name or logo as a trademark, some companies may use an (SM) sign for claiming their right to their name or logo as a service mark. Although closely related, service marks and trademarks differ in some crucial ways. A trademark is used by a business that sells products and a service mark is used by a company that offers services, such as dining or plumbing. Once a mark, either a (TM) or a (SM), is approved by the USPTO, the company selling products and the company offering services use a registered sign usually represented by an R in a circle®.

- **Copyright:** Copyright is a form of intellectual property protection provided by the USPTO. A copyright is a collection of rights that automatically vest to someone who creates an original work of authorship like a literary work, song, movie, or software. These rights include the right to reproduce the work, to prepare derivative works, to distribute copies, and to perform and display the work publicly. The basis for copyright protection stems directly from the United States Constitution. The framers believed that securing the exclusive rights of authors to their writings for limited periods would "promote the progress of science and useful arts." The primary objective of copyright is to induce and reward authors, through the provision of property rights, to create new works and to make those works available to the public to enjoy. The theory is that by granting certain exclusive rights to creators, which allow them to protect their creative works against theft, they receive the benefit of economic reward and the public receives the benefit of the creative works that might not otherwise be created or disseminated.

  There are three basic requirements that a work must meet to be protected by copyright. The work must be:
  - **Original:** To be original, a work must merely be independently created; it cannot be copied from something else. There is no requirement that the work be novel, unique, imaginative or incentive.
  - **Creative:** To satisfy the creativity requirement, a work need only demonstrate a very small amount of creativity. Very few creations fail to satisfy this requirement.

- **Fixed:** To meet the fixation requirement, a work must be fixed in a tangible medium of expression. Protection attaches automatically to an eligible work the moment the work is fixed. A work is considered to be fixed as long as it's sufficiently permanent or stable to permit it be to perceived, reproduced, or otherwise communicated for a period of more than transitory duration.

Generally, a copyrighted work is protected for the length of the author's life plus another 70 years.

- **Trade Secrets:** Trade secrets are another form of intellectual property, and according to the law of most U.S states, a trade secret may consist of any formula, pattern, physical device, idea, process, or compilation of information that both provides the owner of the information with a competitive advantage in the marketplace and is treated in a way that can reasonably be expected to prevent the public or competitors from learning about it. Some examples of potential trade secrets include the formula for an energy drink, recipes for cookies, marketing strategies, manufacturing techniques, computer algorithms, and survey methods used by professional political pollsters.

  Unlike other forms of intellectual property, such as patents, trademarks, and copyrights, which generally require registration in order to be fully effective, trade secrets are essentially a "do-it-yourself" form of protection. You do not register with the USPTO to secure your trade secret; you just keep the information confidential. Trade secret protection lasts for as long as the secret is kept confidential without any statutory limitation period. However, once a trade secret is made available to the public, your trade secret protection ends.

  To treat your intellectual property as a trade secret simply by calling the information a trade secret will not make it a trade secret. A company must affirmatively behave in a way that proves its desire to keep the information secret. This means taking certain precautions over secrecy. The formula for Coca-Cola, perhaps the world's most famous trade secret, is kept locked in a bank vault that can only be opened by a resolution of the Coca-Cola board of directors. Only two Coca-Cola employees ever know the formula at the same time and their identities are never disclosed to the public. You should take reasonable precautions to protect any information you regard as a trade secret. I always advise my clients to use nondisclosure agreements, as the courts have repeatedly reiterated that the use of nondisclosure agreements is the most important way to maintain the secrecy of confidential information.

Your brand is your promise to consumers and the foundation of your business success. In today's business world, protecting your brand is essential to growing your business. Having the proper protection in place for your brand could deter potential infringers from disrupting your business and provide your business with security in the event of infringement.

How Do I Choose a Good Brand Name?

When you first start a business, you don't initially think that the hardest part will be choosing a brand name. However, it doesn't take long before you realize that it is in fact the most challenging aspect. You brand name is an extension of your company. It tells people who you are before they even meet you and it can reinforce the value you provide. The business landscape today is fast paced and extremely competitive. In such an environment, establishing and maintaining a connection between consumers and your brand is more important than ever before. Each bit of competitive edge you can gain counts, including choosing a good brand name for your business. Although developing a brand requires significant time and investment, it will also require figuring out factors to weigh when choosing a brand that's going to be right for your business.

Finding the right brand for your business can have a significant impact on your success. The wrong name can do worse than fail to connect with customers; it can also result in insurmountable business and legal hurdles. In contrast, a clear powerful brand name can be extremely helpful in your marketing and branding efforts. Here are some helpful suggestions on how to come up with a winning brand name for your business:

- **Avoid Hard-to-Spell Names:** Keep it simple. You don't want potential customers getting confused about how to find your business. You want to avoid having to continually correct the misspelled version of your name. Create something short and unique so the name can be easy to remember and keep the name simple so your message can be direct to the point.
- **Don't Limit Your Business Growth:** Picking too narrow a name may cause you problems down the road. Imagine if Jeff Bezos had picked the name "Online Books" instead of "Amazon." You don't want to limit your business to a particular product or a specific city.
- **Conduct Searches:** Once you have determined a brand name you like, the first search you want to conduct is a general web search to see what comes up. Conduct a domain search, and try to secure the ".com" domain name for your business rather than alternatives such as .net, .org, or .biz. Customers tend to associate a .com name with a more established business.

Conduct a trademark search at the USPTO to get an idea as to whether you can get a trademark for the brand name, or to see if any issues arise pertaining to your preferred brand name. Finally, conduct a search on your Secretary of State's website to see if your name is available

- **Meaningful:** What does your company stand for? Today's customers want to interact with companies that have real ethical values and community spirit. Try to decide what you want customers to think about when they're interacting with your company. Creating a brand name with meaning often involves creating images in the minds of your customers. Tie the name to your story.

How Do I Avoid Brand Name Mistakes?

Companies of all sizes routinely underestimate the importance of the naming process. Understandably, business owners want to release their products or services into the marketplace as soon as possible. The problem is that such haphazard decision-making often ends up doing more harm than good. Some common mistakes entrepreneurs make when choosing a brand name are:

- **Rushing the Process:** Choosing the right brand name is complex, as it requires strategy and creativity. Not only do you need to choose a name that is memorable, and not already in use, but you also need to choose a name that can grow with your company. It takes time to choose the right name and by beginning the process early, you could spend time on outlining strategic objectives and brainstorming.
- **Trying to Be Clever:** One of the biggest mistakes made while choosing a name is where you're trying too hard. Choose something too cute and no one will take you seriously. Choose something to complex and no one will remember you. Which is why you should always want to test the name for clarity with family, friends, and potential customers. The easier it is to say, the more likely someone will remember it.
- **Deciding with Emotion:** We all have names that we become attached to for whatever reason. When naming a brand, you should think about what your potentional customers will think and not what you think and remove personal bias from the process.
- **Ignoring Global Meanings:** It happens more often than you would expect. Companies trademark perfectly acceptable brand names only to later realize they mean something completely mortifying in another language. By the time the company realizes their mistake, a difficult decision must be made, either the company overlooks the embarrassing cultural mistake or they pay thousands to rebrand.

Making these mistakes can be very costly and a negative blow to your reputation. Give yourself plenty of time to choose the right name for your brand and go through the exercise of brainstorming, research, and asking your friends who are from other cultures if the name you choose has another meaning in their language. You'll be surprised how much people are willing to help.

Key Takeaways

- Branding, by definition, is a marketing practice in which a company creates a name, symbol, or design that is easily identifiable as belonging to that company. This helps to identify a product or service and distinguish it from other products and services. Branding is important because not only is it what makes a memorable impression on consumers but it allows your customers to know what to expect from your company. It is a way of distinguishing yourself from your competitors and clarifying what it is you offer that makes you the better choice. Your brand is built to be a true representation of who you are as a business and how you wish to be perceived.
- It may not be as well known as Coca-Cola or McDonald's, but your company's brand name is every bit as valuable to you. However, as the internet makes doing business more global than ever, brand names are increasingly at risk of being infringed upon or even stolen, whether purposely or inadvertently. As soon as you create your brand, protect it by taking the right legal measures.
- Picking the right brand name can have a huge impact on your business. It gives your business distinction; it sets you apart from all the other businesses that have similar products or services. Invest some real time in picking your brand the smart way and avoid costly mistakes.

A STORY OF CAUTION FOR STARTUPS

What Happens When Your Startup Doesn't Have Its Legal Ducks in a Row?

You lose $500,000 and a lot more.

As business owners, we are so focused on running the business that we forget to get our legal ducks in a row. Why does it matter? Think about how much you have always wanted to run your own business and how hard you have worked to become your own boss. Now think about how you need money to run your business and keep the doors open. You ask family and friends, and they can't help you. You ask your bank for a loan or a line of credit, and the bank turns you down. Through a lot of heartache, you finally find a private investor who is willing to listen to your story and invest in your business. Here's what can happen if you don't have your legal documents in order.

I received a phone call one day from a client who was very excited about a business investment. This startup was going to be the first in its space to create software that every business eventually would need and buy. This startup needed $500,000 to finish the software, and my client was going to make the investment. Before any money changed hands, we needed to make sure my client's investment would be secure. I sent my due diligence list to the startup asking for corporate documents and ownership percentages for my client. The startup responded by saying it had no corporate documents and no ownership structure was legalized, however, shares were promised to everyone who worked at the startup.

Due to the unpreparedness of the startup, it looked too risky to invest in a business that had no corporate documents or legal contracts with any of the employees. This startup looked less desirable to my client. As any prudent investor would, my client decided not to invest, as the startup was not ready. The startup lost its hard work, hopes and dreams, not to mention $500,000. This happens more often than you think because business owners don't know what they don't know and fail to prepare for these types of situations.

There are a host of legal requirements that must be followed not only at the corporate level but also at the state level. Your company must remain in good standing with the state where it is incorporated. To remain in good standing, states require annual filings and payment of fees, in addition to your company being represented by a registered agent for service of process. However, entities that do not stay on top of their compliance obligations can lose their good standing, and your business will then be considered delinquent, void, suspended, or dissolved. The primary reason a company loses its good standing status is due to not filing its annual reports or paying its franchise tax obligations.

(Continued)

Losing your good standing status can lead to serious consequences, such as:

- **Loss of access to courts:** This may be the most serious consequence, and one that many businesses are not aware of. In many states, a company that is not in good standing may not bring a lawsuit in that state until good standing is restored.
- **Personal liability:** This is the second most serious consequence of losing your good standing with the state. The ability to protect your personal assets is no longer available to you and you can be sued personally by creditors of your company. If your company is not in good standing, the state can hold individual owners of the company personally liable for conducting business on behalf of the company while it was in a delinquent status. These penalties can be severe and levied on each officer, director, or employee who knowingly acted on behalf of the noncompliant company.
- **Difficulties in securing capital and financing:** Most investors and lenders view a loss of good standing as an increased risk and may not invest or approve any financing for your company. Without access to money, your company becomes dangerously close to filing for bankruptcy.
- **Tax liens:** If a company does not pay its franchise tax and loses its good standing status, the taxing authorities can place a tax lien on the company and possibly the owners of the company. Again, lenders will not generally loan money to companies that have tax liens attached to them, as other liens take priority.
- **Fines and penalties:** Some states impose fines and penalties on companies that do not comply with the requirements to maintain a good standing. These can add up quickly and become a burden on the company.

When you are considering incorporating, make sure you do your homework and consider taking the following steps:

- Get advice from a good certified public accountant
- Get help from a good business attorney
- File the paperwork and pay franchise taxes as required
- Obtain the necessary licenses and permits
- Have sufficient capital to run your business

PART 2

Growth Phase

> Without continual growth and progress, such words as improvement, achievement, and success have no meaning.
>
> – Benjamin Franklin

The Rook represents the castle walls, which protect the King, Queen, Bishop, and Knight. The Growth phase represents innovation, as owners try to grow their business with unique confidential ideas and personnel.

CHAPTER 4

How Do I Grow My Small Business?

The Growth phase is an exciting time for any small business. The primary goal of a startup is to get customers, deliver goods, and reach the breakeven point as quickly as possible. However, growing a small business is not easy; it's one of the toughest challenges many face. The success of your small business depends on your efforts to grow profits using various methods. From employee training to marketing, every aspect of your business deserves attention. The focus of your business changes as it moves beyond the Startup phase and into the second phase of your Business Legal Lifecycle®, the Growth phase. The Growth phase can mean so many different things to a business owner, and it can be measured by multiple indicators. Let's first define what growth is for a business.

What Is Growth?

A business dictionary defines business growth as "A phase in the life cycle of an industry when companies move beyond the Startup phase into a phase of increased competition for market share." Another definition provided by the business dictionary is that growth is "The process of improving some measure of an enterprise's success. Business growth can be achieved either by boosting the top line or revenue of the business with greater product sales or service income, or by increasing the bottom line or profitability of the operation by minimizing costs."

Whether you have a hair salon business with a few employees or a software development company with annual revenue in the millions, both companies are likely to face the same common problems at similar stages in their development. Here is the number one most frequently asked question in the Growth phase.

How Do I Grow My Business?

Learning how to grow your business is not just a worthy goal; growing your business is often a necessity for the survival of your business. There are hundreds of growth strategies that are available, but the following growth strategies are the ones that have helped my clients grow their startups:

- **Using Advisors**: Few of us have the breadth of experience and expertise to face all the challenges of a company that wants to grow without relying on some guidance from an engaged and committed advisor. Even the best of us need someone we trust to bounce ideas off, and that's where a good advisory board comes into play. The role of a board is to consult and advise management regarding the strategic and operational direction of the company, ensuring its prosperity. Putting a plan in place for growth with advice from trusted advisors can set your company on the right growth path.
- **Connect with Existing Customers**: When you think about how to grow your business, the first thing that probably comes to mind is getting new customers, but the customers you already have are your best bet for increasing your sales. It's easier and more cost effective to get people who are already buying from you to buy more than to find new customers and persuade them to buy from you.
- **Ask for Referrals**: Attracting new customers to your business is never a bad approach and one of the easiest ways to do it is to ask your current customers for referrals. Having good products and great customer service and assuming that your customers are passing the word about your business is not going to do much to increase your customer base. You have to actively seek referrals. After every sale made to your current customers, ask your customer if they know anyone else who would be interested in your products or services.
- **Publish Newsletters**: One of the most effective ways to stay on top of your customer's mind is through email marketing. Email marketing allows you to target particular groups of customers or even specific individuals. Offering individual customers special birthday deals on products or services is one way to engage with them, making them feel "special," which could lead to referrals to their family and friends. This kind of personalization helps a business gradually develop and maintain a relationship with their customers that can lead to increased sales and customer loyalty.

- **Public Speaking**: Public speaking allows you to showcase your knowledge, skills, and expertise. If you craft your presentation strategically, you will accomplish a few goals including building trust, sharing value, providing insight into the benefits you are offering, and highlighting customer successes. The more you get exposure, the more you'll develop a following and the more people will want to buy from you.
- **Hire Great Employees**: If you want to expand your business, finding employees with specific skills, such as sales, accounting, or IT, should be a top priority. Searching for new talent is a good problem to have because it means your company is on the growth path. Hiring employees is definitely an investment, but hiring the wrong employees will cost you more money in the long run. Be more selective and take your time finding the right fit for your business.
- **Enter New Markets**: There are several ways of growing your business by making your product or service available to a new pool of customers. This can be achieved by either expanding your business to a new location, if you have a storefront, or offering your product or service virtually through your website by adding an e-commerce site where customers can buy your products online. Another approach is to extend your reach through advertising. Once you have identified a new market, you might advertise in select media that target that market. If your new market consists of a younger demographic, you may want to use social media for advertising your products, such as through Instagram.
- **Create a Niche Market**: Remember the analogy of the big fish in the small pond? That's essentially how this strategy for growing your business works. The niche market is the pond – a narrowly defined group of customers. Think of them as a subset of the larger market whose needs are not being met, and concentrate on meeting those needs. An advertising company, for instance, might focus only on helping law firms, while a dog food company might specialize in creating food for senior dogs.
- **Create Strategic Partnerships**: Creating an alliance or strategic partnership with another business can have a tremendous impact on the growth for both companies. It can be especially beneficial and cost saving for a small business. The right partnerships will help your business gain a competitive advantage and give your business exposure to a new pool of customers.
- **Consider Franchising**: A franchise is a business in which the owners or "franchisors" sell the rights to their business name, logo, and processes to independent third parties to operate, called "franchisees," in exchange for royalties. Some examples of well-known franchises include McDonald's, Subway, UPS, and H & R Block.

Can Rapid Growth Be Bad?

How and when to grow are key decisions that every small business must face eventually. In startup mode, growing too slowly means you risk running out of the capital needed to support the basic operational costs before sales reach the breakeven point. Growing too quickly means you face another set of challenges, ones that put you at a greater risk.

As an entrepreneur, you dream of the day when you've got a steady stream of customers or clients eager to work with you. But what happens when the workload becomes more than you can handle? As far as problems go, this might sound like a great one to have. However, rapid, uncontrolled business expansion can have negative repercussions in the short as well as the long run. In fact, the result is often the same, failure. You might be thinking, this makes no sense. It sounds counterintuitive, because businesses exist to make more money and grow with the passage of time. While expansion is always good, what smart business owners and entrepreneurs should look and strive for is "controlled expansion."

Working with entrepreneurs and small business owners over the years, I've watched companies go from small to stellar thanks to a well-managed growth strategy, and have witnessed an equal number implode seemingly overnight in an attempt to keep up with the pressures of demands. I've complied some telltale signs that indicate your business is growing too fast and could potentially be heading for failure.

- **Cash Flow Crunch**: One of the first telltale symptoms of unsustainable growth is a clogged cash flow. While the demand for your products or services might be high, your business cash flow is lagging behind. A cash flow crunch can create a host of other issues and is a common concern for businesses. Some of the unmistakable signs of cash flow issues include:
  - **Multiple outstanding invoices**: When unpaid invoices start stacking up, it's easy for those outstanding payments to fall through the cracks. Although you have plenty of demand, your customers not paying on time can leave you in the lurch when it comes to working capital.
  - **Missed payments to vendors**: Dropping the ball when paying your vendors is a definitive sign of cash flow issues, especially when you need to wait for your invoices to be paid in order to pay your vendors. Not all vendors are understanding and could refuse to do business with you until they are paid.
  - **Messy financial systems**: While you may have mastered the basics of payroll and accounts receivable, the bigger your business, the more complicated your financials become. The more work you have coming in,

the harder it is to keep track of sales, invoicing, and expenses without an accounting system that works for your business.

As your business and revenue grow, make sure you have the tracking and execution you need to make your money matters simpler. That might mean taking some time to assess your current finances, putting new systems in place, and potentially outsourcing these tasks to a professional. Upgrade your financial tools to ensure you can track your expenses, complete payroll, send invoices, and collect payments.

- **Operational Inefficiency**: When your business starts growing quickly, you will be forced to improvise to manage increased demand for your products or services. Rapid growth can render your business processes and systems useless due to lack of proper infrastructure. When business buildup happens too fast and too soon, you will not be able to adhere to your perfect business plan where your operational processes flow smoothly. You may be pressured to hire more people sooner than you anticipated and you may not be skilled in choosing the right people or you may not have the time to design your workflow to accommodate increased demand. Unprepared rapid growth, while supporting inefficient operations, could result in these problems:
  - Your new employees are poorly trained.
  - You can't manufacture or buy inventory quickly enough to fill orders.
  - You haven't accurately determined the cost of delivering your products or dealing with customers.
  - Your customer service is nonexistent.
- **Lack of Space**: As your business grows, the number of employees and desks and the amount of inventory you keep on hand are likely to increase too. If you outgrow your office space and to move to a new location before your lease is up, you could be responsible for continuing to pay for your old lease until a new tenant is found for the space. The best way to avoid this problem is to plan for it when you are signing a lease for commercial space.

  If you're just starting out, you may want to opt for an executive suite or space in a business center that you rent by the month or year. If your business is at the point where it makes sense to sign a more permanent lease, then you'll probably want to limit the term of your lease to 3 years if you expect to be growing more. If possible, have your attorney negotiate an "out" clause in the lease. This is a clause that would spell out terms under which you could end the lease early, such as by giving the landlord three months' written notice. If you are already in a lease that does not have an out clause and you need more space, ask your landlord if there are other available spaces that can meet your growing needs.
- **Hiring**: The balance you are able to create within your small team of great people is part of the magic behind how an excellent startup happens. When

growing your business, it's only natural that you would expand your team. However, as you grow, it becomes difficult to keep hiring people who check every box while also filling your needs as quickly as possible. Hiring new talent can help you solve big problems within your business, and strategic hiring can help you scale sustainably. When your business is growing at a rapid pace, it can be tempting to hire on the fly just to have an extra set of hands. But hiring without a plan can lead to bringing on new employees without the right experience or with values that don't align with yours. It usually takes about three months to train and about a $4,000 investment to bring on a new employee. All that time and expense is a waste if a hastily hired employee is a poor fit and leaves within six months. This can also lower your current employees' morale and waste valuable training time.

Create a strategic hiring plan that focuses on smart talent acquisition, onboarding and training, and retaining all those great employees you hire. When creating your hiring plan, consider these factors:

- **Prioritize hiring for specific positions**: What teams need support the most? Which are understaffed? And where will a new hire make the biggest impact?
- **Weigh hiring versus outsourcing**: Assess whether a part-time employee or a freelancer could fill the gaps to get your business through this high growth period. Does it make sense to outsource certain tasks, like marketing?
- **Hire for potential as well as experience**: Sometimes the best person for the job just hasn't started doing the work yet. Make sure that when you're hiring, you're looking at the potential growth of new hires, not just their experience.
- **Promote internally**: Rather than look outward for talent, it often makes more sense to hire from within. Training and general investment in current employees can increase engagement, boost productivity, and lead to higher retention. Share opportunities with current employees to promote and take pride as an employee, as well as experience new challenges.
- **Constant Customer Complaints**: Demand is high, your to-do lists are long, and your employees are multitasking. A few customer complaints occasionally are part of doing business, but when negative feedback starts to pile up, it is an indication that you are not meeting client expectations. When you're too busy to give your customers the service they deserve, they'll notice. This could be due to lack of personnel to manage client interactions. It could also hint at other issues if your staff is spread too thin and is cutting corners to meet customer demand. Clients who provide positive feedback are bound to be repeat customers. A host of negative feedback could indicate that you are unable to cope with the market's expectations in terms

of the delivery because you are overwhelmed. Make sure to monitor your feedback system regularly, keep an eye on social media mentions of your business, and have a plan in place for handling both positive and negative feedback. Without additional support, important tasks like customer service can fall through the cracks.

- **Overworked Employees**: A vibrant workplace inspires employees to work their hardest, but when work consumes most of their waking hours, you run the risk of losing your trained and trusted employees. If your business is growing uncontrollably, naturally a large proportion of that burden will be borne by your employees. To keep up, they might find themselves working late. This usually results in a dip in productivity and a rise in employee turnover, both of which can negatively affect your business. You may find yourself busy hiring and training new staff when other, more important aspects of your business need your attention. Pay attention to the evolving workplace culture as your business grows and find the time to discuss quality of life issues during staff meetings, creating an environment where your employees feel valued and cared for.

When your business is growing too quickly, you likely focus on making it from one day to the next. When you're focused on checking items off your to-do list, you're simply surviving in the present. That leaves little time to shift your focus from just surviving right now to how you can thrive in the future. It's tough to nail down important long-term goals for your business, or even envision what you want for your business 5 or 10 years down the road. Without a clear vision of the future, it's easy for your business to go off the rails while you're sprinting to keep up with your exponential growth. This is where looking back at your business plan will help guide you back on track and keep the important things in perspective.

How Can I Measure My Business Growth?

New business owners have numerous goals when they're starting out, including growth. One way to measure the growth of your business is by using milestones. There are ways to reach growth milestones that can help catapult a business to success, but the main focus should always be on reducing your risks, which are attached to the growth milestones. Here are some risks and solutions related to milestones that will help you grow your business or prepare it for growth in the right way:

- **Milestone 1 – Hire the right people**: Before you can even think about your company's growth trajectory, you need to ensure that you have a solid staff that can help you achieve the right growth for your business. Having the right employees is critical to the success of any business. Good employees can follow instructions, present new ideas, and motivate other employees to work hard. They are dedicated, conscientious, trustworthy, and do not need to be micromanaged. Conversely, the wrong employees can not only slow down or impede the progress of your business but also can cause you to lose money through wasted training time, improperly performed tasks, and even stealing. Furthermore, any incompetence or improper activities by your employees can reflect poorly upon you and your business.

Before hiring anyone, you should familiarize yourself with the laws and regulations imposed regarding soliciting and interviewing employees. Protecting employee rights, ensuring physical safety, and maintaining fair treatment are at the heart of most laws created to safeguard the hiring process. Laws protect against discrimination on the grounds of race, color, religion, national origin, age, sex, or disability. They also protect against sexual harassment and unfair treatment of employees. You not only need to be aware of such employment laws, you also need to protect your business by establishing appropriate policies for your company. Here are some suggestions you could start with:

- **Reducing the Risk – Have the right contracts in place**: When hiring employees, a business needs a number of documents in order to reduce its risk. Some of these must-have employment documents are:
  - Employee Handbook, which is always kept up-to-date with changes in the law. An employee handbook is a compilation of the policies, procedures, working conditions, and behavioral expectations that guide employee actions in a particular workplace.
  - Nondisclosure Agreements, to keep your trade secrets from being shared with the world. A nondisclosure agreement is a legal contract that prohibits someone from sharing information deemed confidential.
  - Employee Application, which will save you time gathering background information. An application for employment is a form that asks candidates information about themselves to gauge whether they are a good fit for a job.
  - Employee Contract, which defines the professional relationship between you and your employees. An employee contract is a written legal document that spells out binding terms between the employee and the employer, listing the rights, responsibilities, and obligations of both parties.
  - Invention Assignment Agreement, so any inventions that your employees create while working for you will belong to your company. An invention assignment agreement is a contract that gives the employer

certain rights to inventions created or conceptualized by the employee during the employment relationship.

- Independent Contractor Agreement, which helps secure the work you just paid for and assure that the work product belongs to your company. An independent contractor agreement is a written contract that spells out the terms of the working arrangement between a contractor and client.

   Establishing appropriate company policies may help reduce the risk of litigation.

- **Milestone 2 – Never take your eye off the money**: When your business is smaller, you probably have a pretty good command of your financial numbers. You're able to watch your cash flow and know fairly quickly how expenses are stacking up to revenue. But once you start growing, it becomes harder to keep track of your financials. There are a number of financial implications you need to take into consideration. Start with understanding your cash flow and then creating a budget for your business. Things to keep in mind:

  - **Reducing the Risk – Hire Professionals**: Money will always be the telltale of your business. That is why it is extremely important to hire the right accountant. You need someone who knows how to work with fast-growing businesses and can provide you with profit and loss statements, so you know where your business stands at all times. Your accountant will be privy to confidential information and may have access to your bank accounts. When hiring this person, you will need to have an independent contractor agreement or a services agreement in place, which will include confidentiality language. You may want this person to provide you with evidence of liability insurance, which is an additional security measure for your money.

- **Milestone 3 – Collecting your money**: A big challenge fast-growing companies can face is that their accounts receivable accumulates faster than their sales or their ability to collect. The company's growing, but is it selling on account and not collecting fast enough? Here is a suggestion that can help reduce the risk:

  - **Reducing the Risk – Have a solid customer contract in place**: Having a solid contract with your customers is critical for a fast-growing business. The contract should lay out the terms of when and how you will get paid. This is usually where misunderstandings occur; therefore, payment terms need to be clearly spelled out in the contract and again in your invoice, if you use an invoice to receive payment. The phrasing in the contract should indicate that payment should be made in a timely manner, for example, payment is due upon receipt of invoice or payment is due within 15 or 30 days from the date of the invoice. If using your customer's contract, beware of language that promises payment after the invoice is approved, which could mean that you may wait for someone to approve an invoice because they are on vacation, or there might be a dispute and you have to wait until the dispute is addressed. Your contract should have language that allows the payment of the undisputed part of the invoice so you're not waiting a long time for money you have earned. Make sure the customer contract has language that allows for charging rush fees and passing along costs associated with delays caused by the customer. The faster you grow, the more money you will need and getting paid on time can save you thousands in loan fees and interest. Having a solid customer contract in place can help reduce the risk that you will fall behind on collections.

What Tools Can I Use to Monitor My Growing Business?

Often as a business owner, you become so focused on bringing products or services to market and advertising them, you fail to grow all aspects of the business. As a result, while the business is growing in sales, the infrastructure is not keeping pace with business growth. Flaws in management systems begin to show, and quality control is not in sync with the growth. Eventually, you reach a tipping point in which these flaws cause the system to collapse.

Here are some tools that you can utilize that will grow your organizational structure in proportion to your business:

- **Create a Scalable Management Model**: As your business grows, you must develop scalable management and quality-control systems. In the beginning, management and quality control are easy, as everyone knows what everyone else's role is in the company. As your business grows and duties become more segmented among new employees, you must put a management structure in place to ensure accountability against established benchmarks as well as to make sure quality control of your goods and services remains constant. Each position's duties and responsibilities should be defined in writing. An organizational chart should be created that defines who is responsible for what, who reports to whom, and how often.
- **Define a Quality-Control System**: As your company grows, you must ensure that the quality of your goods or services is maintained despite its increasing size. You must determine what elements belong in a quality control system and then assign the responsibility of maintaining that quality to someone within your management model.

- **Use Professionals**: You should have the following people on your team to ensure your business is growing in the right way, with the right procedures and the right oversight:
  - Hire a really good business attorney
  - Employ a really good accountant
  - Use a reputable payroll company
  - Create internal policies on hiring and firing employees
  - Set a company culture and lead by example

Key Takeaways

- Learning how to grow your business is not just a worthy goal; growing your business is often a necessity for the survival of your business. Use suggested strategies to grow your business in the right way.
- Growing too quickly means you face another set of challenges, ones that put you at a greater risk. Understand the telltale signs of rapid growth and how to best minimize the risk. Set milestones in place to guide you with the growth of your company. It's always great practice to plan for growth and not just stumble across it.
- Hire professionals who can help with the growth of your business. Don't try to do it all by yourself. You don't know what you don't know. This is the best single act you can do for your company to ensure success.

CHAPTER 5

How Do I Manage My Growing Business?

Experiencing a period of rapid business growth can be an exhilarating time for your company. Revenue is increasing, profits are high, and you're making a name for yourself among your competitors. However, properly managing business growth and realizing the full benefits in a growth environment are not simple tasks. If you start a Growth phase in your business it is usually because you have done something right. A new product or service has been launched, marketing has been effective, sales are coming in, and you're delivering efficiently. This cycle will continue for a while, but as you take on more customers to feed the growth, you will at some point reach the limit of your business capacity. Being able to ride the successes in a business Growth phase is crucial. If you start to show signs that you can't cope with the new demand, then your business can recede as quickly as it grew. It is important to manage your growing company effectively.

The second most frequently asked question in the Growth phase is how to manage a growing business.

How Do I Manage My Growing Business?

No business can afford to leave its growth to chance. Businesses need a consistent plan that incorporates their vision for growth. Fast growth is not always easy to handle, but a proactive step-by-step approach can help make it more manageable. Here are some steps you can take to manage your business:

- **Define your Growth Objectives:** Be strategic about your growth. It's a good exercise to first ask yourself some very basic questions in order to determine your key objectives:

- Do I have the necessary capital to finance my growth?
- Do I have cash flow problems or am I managing well?
- Do I have assets available at hand that I could turn into cash if needed?
- Am I expanding too quickly?
- Am I growing because I want to be more profitable or is it uncontrolled growth?
- Am I hiring too fast?
- Am I collecting my receivables fast enough?
- Is my inventory in line with my growth?
- Does my management team have the right competencies to handle the growth?

Your business objectives are the results you hope to achieve and maintain as you run and grow your business. As a business owner, you are concerned with every aspect of your business and need to have clear goals in mind for your company. Having a comprehensive list of business objectives creates the guidelines that become the foundation of your business. Consider some of the following growth objectives you should spend time defining:

- **Profitability:** making sure that revenue stays ahead of the costs of doing business.
- **Productivity:** investing in employee training, equipment, and the overall resources your company needs for growth.
- **Customer Service:** good customer service helps you retain clients and generate repeat revenue. Keeping your customers happy should be a primary objective of your company as you grow.
- **Core Values:** your company's mission statement is a description of the core values of your company. It is necessary to create a positive corporate culture.
- **Marketing:** understanding your customer buying trends, anticipating product needs, and developing business partners that help your company improve its market dominance.
- **Prepare a Growth Strategy:** A growth strategy is a plan of action that allows you to achieve a higher level of market share than you currently have. Growth can be achieved by practices like adding new locations, investing in customer acquisition, or expanding a product line. A company's industry and target market influence which growth strategies it will choose. Typically, there are four types of growth strategies and you might use one or all of the following:
  - **Product Development Strategy:** growing your market share by developing new products, as these new products should either solve a new problem within your industry or add to the existing problem your current products solve.

- **Market Development Strategy:** growing your market share by developing new segments of the market, expanding your user base, or expanding your current users' usage of your product.
- **Market Penetration Strategy:** growing your market share by bundling products, lowering prices, and advertising, everything you can do through marketing after your product is created.
- **Diversification Strategy:** growing your market share by entering entirely new markets.

Here are somes growth strategy examples used by some well-known companies:

- **Dropbox:** As a trailblazer in the cloud storage software arena, Dropbox launched in 2008 and introduced the world to the ease of keeping files in the cloud, rather than on a physical device. The strategy used was product development strategy – they allowed people to try their product, they offered a valuable incentive to share it with others, those people accept and share with their network, new users sign up, see the incentive for themselves, and share with their networks.
- **Harry's:** You might remember when Dollar Shave Club burst on the scene in 2012 with the promise of high quality, affordable blades delivered right to your door. Harry's followed suit the next year by utilizing the market penetration strategy.
- **WhatsApp:** When entering a crowded marketplace, you've got to stand out. Your value proposition needs to clearly demonstrate your competitive advantage over others. Why should users go with your product or service instead of someone else's? WhatsApp wasn't the first cross platform message app when it launched in 2009, but it has gone on to become one of the most successful. The founders, Brian Acton and Jan Koum, wanted to create a product without the baggage that came with similar apps at the time. They intentionally opted for no ads, no marketing, and a free first year to attract users fed up with other providers. They used the market development strategy and created a product that was brilliantly simple for sending and receiving instant messages.
- **Forecast Your Cash Requirements:** Running out of cash is not only a sign of poor planning, but it's also one of the biggest reasons that businesses fail. Forecasting your company's cash flow can be tricky because of the many variables that determine how much cash you will need for operations versus the amount available. Understanding and predicting cash flow is the key to keeping track of your purse strings and ensuring you don't overspend. While there is no magic formula available to solve every company's cash flow forecasting, having the right processes in place is a good start. What and how you measure something will vary depending on

your business, industry, and goals. For example, a seasonal business that generates 80% of its sales over just three months of the year will have different cash flow needs than one whose revenue is steadier throughout the year. Forecast your cash requirements by doing an analysis of your cash inflow and outflow. This will enable you to determine future cash requirements. Knowing this, you can look at your current financial situation and assess if you can make improvements. You may be able to get additional financing for working capital, restructure your debt or convert unused assets into cash. A cash flow forecast may include the following sections:

- **Operating Cash:** the cash on hand that you have to work with at the start of a given period. For a monthly projection, this is the cash balance available at the start of a month.
- **Revenue:** depending on the type of business, revenue may include estimated sales figures, tax refunds or grants, loan payments received, or incoming fees. The revenue section covers the total sources of cash for each month.
- **Expenses:** cash outflows may include your salary and other payroll costs, business loan payments, rent, asset purchases, and other expenditures.
- **Net Cash Flow:** the closing cash balance, which reveals whether you have excess funds or a deficit.

- **Control Costs:** Cost control is the practice of identifying and reducing business expenses to increase profits. Controlling your costs should become a priority and just as important as increasing your company's revenues. This is why performing an internal evaluation of expenses and understanding how your processes function is the best path to identifying unnecessary costs and establishing an efficient program that will offer sustained benefits for your business. Here are some tips that will help in establishing some internal processes for cost cutting:
  - **Prepare a Budget:** When creating a budget, make sure that it's flexible and not something you produce at the beginning of the year to not be referred to again. A dynamic budget reviewed regularly can help you to react to ever-changing market climates. It'll let you know when it's time to invest in more marketing to expand or cut costs when faced with unexpected revenue drops.
  - **Measure Your Costs:** Before you create an action plan to reduce your costs, you should create an evaluation of your company's expenses and analyses and list your expenses from the most relevant to the least relevant. The analysis will allow you to identify many hidden costs that are certainly affecting your company's results.

- **Make Short-Term, Medium-Term, and Long-Term Analysis:** To take assertive control of your expenses and reduce costs, it's important to visualize your reductions over the short-term, medium-term, and long-term. To do this, evaluate alternatives that will reduce your costs over a longer time frame.

- **Improve Process Management:** Evaluating only ledger accounts or costs is not enough to identify potential bottlenecks and problems in your company's processes. Therefore, when thinking about processes, many activities are revealed such as rework, duplication, or processes and actions carried out with low value for the company. Since controlling and reducing costs are tasks that require information, you need to pay attention to internal processes.

- **Renegotiate Contracts:** Each year or at the end of your contract terms, make sure to review the terms and negotiate with your current supplier or shop around for a better deal. A smart way is to not have a contract life exceed one year, forcing your supplier to negotiate renewal terms. Do your research and find at least three quotes for anything you buy or sign, as this can make negotiating with suppliers easier. Although this may seem time-consuming, it could save you on substantial costs in the long run. Something that goes hand in hand with renegotiating contracts is settling invoices early. This is a simple way to cut costs, as many suppliers often offer incentives and discounts for clients who settle their invoices early. This can help to improve your cash flow.

- **Outsource Services:** there is no reason for a business to absorb hiring and payroll related costs from non-company related services. Therefore, when working with outsourced labor, the company gains efficiency and feels confident that they are working with a partner who knows how to get the job done correctly.

- **Refinancing:** After analyzing your company, you will be better able to examine your payment procedures. Refinancing can help reduce your monthly payments by rescheduling your debts and spreading your payments over a longer period. Some financial institutions provide business loans to refinance debt for businesses undergoing rapid expansion, purchasing equipment, or increasing financial flexibility.

For any small business owner, one of the top goals is to eventually grow. Whether this means bringing in more clients, branching into new markets, or operating with a team of employees, the process is the same. If you start the Growth phase in your business, it is usually because you've done something right. So, what could possibly go wrong?

What Could Go Wrong?

Unfortunately, too many businesses never make it to the Growth phase, sometimes as a result of mistakes they make while trying to get to the next level. As you work hard to run your fast-growing business, more often than not, you'll forget to ask yourself, "What could go wrong?" At some point in your business, usually when all is going smoothly, you will encounter certain pitfalls. If you want to give your business the best chance of success, it's important to be aware of the most common mistakes and how to avoid them. Knowing the potential pitfalls in advance and understanding how to mitigate them can be the fine line between success and failure. Here are some major pitfalls you could experience as you are growing your business:

- **Insufficient Capital:** If you want to continue to thrive as a business, you'll need to have the funds in place to finance your operations. Whether this means landing a round of investment dollars, taking out a small business loan, or simply bringing in enough revenue from your work to pay the bills, it's important to have a budget to support what you're doing. The biggest mistake you can make is in growing so fast that you have more money going out than coming in. For that reason, you'll likely need to set aside cash reserves for at least 5 to 6 months before taking that next step.

  For any business, a detailed monthly budget is crucial. This budget should be refined as your business progresses, based on real data. Over time, you'll develop an intimate knowledge of the inner workings of your operations and this will put you in the position of making decisions about how many expenses your business can handle. If you are not good with finances, one of the best investments you can make is in a skilled bookkeeper or accountant who can help you get an expert view of what your budget can withstand.

- **Failure to Use Professionals:** Most business owners mistakenly believe they can do everything on their own. They do everything from writing their own contracts to doing their own accounting, handling clients, and finding new deals. This mind-set is a huge mistake; although tackling each project on your own is a good way to learn the ins and outs of your business, in the end, all you are doing is crippling your progress, your productivity, and, ultimately, the success of your business. Learn to hire professionals, such as a business attorney and an accountant, put together a management team, and delegate the work to efficient people better skilled in those areas, so you can do what you do best: run your company.

- **Losing Key Employees:** Loss of key employees can occur in many ways. They can quit, they can retire, they can move out of town, or they can pass on. Your business could suffer significantly if any of these occur and you have no procedures or descriptions of the tasks that the key employee performed. To avoid such disaster, consider putting the following in place:

- Create operations manuals
- Write job descriptions
- Document extraordinary tasks
- Cross-train
- **Spreading Your Management Team Too Thin:** It's very easy for a fast-growing company to assign too many tasks to the management team. Before you know it, the management team is stretched too thin. Having a simple plan and being able to prioritize and supervise your management team at a higher level can control the pressure on your team. Provide your team a clear plan, with each item assigned to someone. List timelines or milestones for that person to follow. Give everyone involved a copy of the plan so they all stay on track and accomplish the tasks assigned to them before taking on more tasks. Your management team will thank you.
- **Dependence:** Too many companies fail because they were overly dependent on one thing. Maybe that's a highly valuable customer. Maybe it's a very talented and experienced worker. Maybe it's just an environmental condition that allows for the company to be successful. Customers can opt out. Workers can quit. Environmental conditions can and will change. If you allow any part of your business to be dependent on anything, you're setting yourself up for disaster. Instead, hedge your bets by investing in multiple variations and multiple complementary dependencies.

By no means are these pitfalls intended to cover every possible disaster that could befall your company. There are plenty of other dangers that could weaken your brand or compromise your internal structure, but these are some of the most common and some of the most preventable. As the leader of your company, your sight needs to be focused on the distant horizon, not on the small day-to-day problems that almost always work themselves out naturally. Keep watch for these encroaching hazards and take immediate actions to resolve them before they become irreversible.

Key Takeaways

- No business can afford to leave its growth to chance. Businesses need a consistent plan that incorporates their vision for growth. Fast growth is not always easy to handle, but a proactive step-by-step approach can help make it more manageable. Create a plan for growth with the input of your management team.

- Unfortunately, too many businesses never make it to the Growth phase, sometimes as a result of mistakes they make while trying to get to the next level. As you work hard to run your fast-growing business, more often than not, you'll forget to ask yourself, "What could go wrong?" Having a clear understanding of the pitfalls that can be preventable goes a long way.
- Hire the right professionals to help you with your business. As I have said before, you don't know what you don't know. Don't try to save a few dollars by doing it yourself. This is the worst thing you can do for your business. Be smart and delegate.

CHAPTER 6

How Do I Get Funding for My Growing Business?

Accounting for more than 99% of all U.S. businesses, according to the Census Bureau, small businesses are the backbone of the country's economy and job market. They create many products and services used on a daily basis by consumers and other companies. During the life of almost any business, the owner will need to seek money to help with its growth or to keep it going through a rough patch.

The third most frequently asked question in the Growth phase is how to obtain funding.

How Do I Get Funding for My Growing Business?

There are two ways to externally fund a business: debt and equity. When debt is used, the investor receives a note for his or her cash. The note spells out the terms of repayment, including timing and interest. The benefit of using debt is that you retain ownership of your company. The downside is that you have an obligation to repay. If you fail to meet your commitment, the lender, under certain circumstances, can force the company into liquidation.

Then there's equity. An owner who uses equity to fund a business turns over an ownership stake to an investor in return for cash. The benefit is that there is no obligation to repay the investor. The downside is the owner has to give up a part of the company. This can entail losing some control over your business.

There are many different sources of equity and debt funding. Below are some examples of how you can utilize and implement the equity in your business to fund your growing company.

Equity Funding

- **Bootstrapping**: The business funds itself. When first getting started, or growing, many entrepreneurs use bootstrapping, which means financing your company by scraping together any personal funds you can find. This typically includes your savings account, credit cards, and any home equity lines you may have. In many cases, using the money you have instead of borrowing or raising is a great approach, and some business owners continue to bootstrap until their business becomes profitable.
- **Family and Friends**: Asking your family and friends for money might seem like a daunting prospect, but tapping those closest to you is often a good first step, as they can provide either equity or debt funding. While this may initially seem like a good source, be careful about selling part of your business to this group. Unfortunately, businesses fail and the loss of capital can then cause hurt feelings, ruin friendships, and make for very unpleasant family gatherings. Be sure that your investors (friends and family) know the true risks involved when giving or loaning money to your company.
- **Partners**: Taking on a partner can be a source of funding. An ideal partner comes with strong connections, relevant experience, and valuable advice, not just financial support. Before adding a partner to your business, you may want to consider, what is your new vision for your company and does the prospective partner share that same perspective? Not only is it important that you both share the vision for the overall goals and objectives for the company, it's also important to come to an agreement on which actionable steps will be required to execute the vision.
- **Angel Investors**: An angel investor is a person or group who invests in a new or small business venture, providing capital for startup or expansion. Angel investors are typically individuals who have spare cash available and are looking for a higher rate of return than would be given by more traditional investments. An angel investor typically looks for a return of 25% or more. Angel investment is a form of equity financing where the investor supplies funding in exchange for taking an equity position in your company. The big advantage is that financing from angel investment is much less risky than debt financing. Unlike a loan, invested capital does not have to be paid back in the event of business failure, and most angel investors understand business, can take that risk of losing their investment, and take a long-term view.

- **Venture Capital**: Venture capital is a form of financing that provides funds to early state, emerging companies with high growth potential in exchange for equity or an ownership stake in your company. Venture capitalists take the risk of investing in companies with the hope that they will earn significant returns when the companies become successful. They are wealthy enough to take losses that may be incurred by investing in unproven, high-risk companies. When choosing companies to invest in, they consider the company's growth potential, the strength of its management team, and the uniqueness of its products or services. Venture capitalists provide funding in exchange for control of decision-making and a portion of your company's ownership.
- **Crowdfunding**: Crowdfunding is a way to raise funds for a specific cause or project by asking a large number of people to donate money, usually in small amounts, and usually during a relatively short period of time, such as a few months. Crowdfunding is done online, often with social networks, which make it easy for supporters to share with their social networks. Organizations, businesses, and individuals alike can use crowdfunding for any type of project, for example, to support the growth of a new product line, creative projects, business startups, charitable causes, or personal expenses. There are two main types of crowdfunding. One is donation-based funding, where donors contribute to a total amount for a new project, which allows you to develop the product or service. The other type of crowdfunding is investment crowdfunding, where businesses seeking capital sell ownership stakes online in the form of equity or debt. In this model, individuals who fund become owners or shareholders and have a potential for financial return.

Debt Funding

- **Small Business Administration (SBA) Loan**: The SBA is a federal agency dedicated to helping entrepreneurs improve their small businesses, take advantage of contracting opportunities, and gain access to business funding. The SBA does not directly loan money to businesses, but it increases the chance that your small business will be approved for loans by guaranteeing all or part of the loan. These guarantees provide a bigger incentive for lenders to approve loans for small businesses by easing their anxieties. There are three main SBA loan programs, which help a wide variety of small businesses obtain debt financing:
  - **7(a) Loan Program**: The most common of the SBA programs, this offers the most open-ended terms and qualifications, making it suited for a wide variety of businesses. Through this program, borrowers can access

up to $5 million in funds for working capital, equipment, and real estate purchases.

- **Microloan Program**: Many solopreneurs struggle with access to debt financing because the loan sizes they typically need don't meet most lenders' lower limits. To address this challenge, the SBA created the microloan program, which provide opportunities for entrepreneurs in need of funding of between $500 and $50,000. The average microloan amount is about $14,000. These loans are designed for businesses that have never before received a bank loan and have low or nonexistent business credit history.
- **CDC/504 Loan Program**: This program is designed for businesses looking to make a major fixed asset purchase, such as large equipment, land improvements, or the purchase or renovation of an existing building. Borrowers through this program can take out up to $5 million with repayment terms of up to 20 years.
- **Term Loans**: A traditional term loan is the easiest type of debt financing to understand because it's probably what you naturally think of when you think of a business loan. The terms are pretty simple; you borrow a fixed amount of money, usually for a specifically stated business purpose. Then you pay back the loan over a fixed term and typically at a fixed interest rate. If you're looking for a loan with a fixed interest rate and predictable monthly payments that can be used for a wide range of business purposes, a term loan will likely be your first and most obvious choice.
- **Business Line of Credit**: A business line of credit is perhaps the most flexible form of business funding available, as it gives you capital to draw upon to meet a variety of business needs. Once established, you may draw on your line of credit as you would a personal credit card. You can use this capital for whatever your business needs, such as to buy inventory, handle seasonal cash flows, or pay off other business debts.
- **Equipment Financing**: Applying for an equipment loan can be a quick streamlined way to access funds to purchase computers, machinery, vehicles, or virtually any other type of equipment for your business. The equipment itself acts as collateral for the loan.
- **Invoice Financing**: If delayed payments from clients are seriously endangering your cash flow, invoice financing is a great option to get your receivables back on track. Also known as accounts receivable financing, invoice financing is a system in which companies buy your accounts receivable. Invoice financing is also known as factoring, which is a finance method where a company sells its receivables at a discount to get cash up front. It's often used by companies with poor credit or by businesses such as apparel manufacturers that have to fill orders long before they get paid.

- **Merchant Cash Advance**: A merchant cash advance is a lump sum payment of liquid capital. A lender will offer it to a business in exchange for a percentage of the company's future sales. When a borrower receives cash from a merchant capital provider, the borrower agrees to pay back the cash advance, plus a fee, by allowing the provider to automatically deduct an agreed-upon percentage of the borrower's company's daily sales.
- **Your 401(k)**: If you have a 401(k) either from a previous job or you have one set up for your company, those funds you've accumulated over the years may be used to help grow your business. The tax code provisions actually allow you to tap into your 401(k) without paying a penalty if you follow the right steps. The steps are simple enough but legally complex, so you'll need someone with experience setting up a C Corporation and the appropriate retirement plan to roll your retirement assets into. Remember that you're investing your retirement funds, which means if things don't go as planned, you could lose your nest egg.

How Do I Keep Growing My Business?

Those who have survived Startup and are successfully managing a growing business may be wondering how to take the next step and grow the business beyond its current status. Like it or not, your business expenses go up each year, and to stay profitable, your business needs to grow so it can absorb those increases. There are numerous possibilities; choosing the proper one for your business will depend on the type of business you own; your available resources; and how much money, time, and sweat equity you are willing to invest all over again.

Here are some actions you can take that can help you keep moving your business forward:

- **Fat Trimming**: There are two types of growth, top line growth and bottom line growth. Top line growth is an actual increase in revenue. Bottom line growth is the trimming of expenses allowing you to keep more of your earned revenue. As businesses grow, they often try new ideas, hire new people, and purchase new equipment. Much of it is likely to produce revenue but some areas of your business might cost more than the revenue they produce. This is where you'll do an analysis of your company by answering questions such as, do you have an employee who isn't contributing to your company's revenue? Rework their job description or let them go. Do you have equipment sitting gathering dust? Put it to work or sell it. Do you subscribe to various online services that you do not use? Cancel them. Bottom line growth is often the easiest way to increase margins because it doesn't rely on finding new customers. Keep more of your revenue as profit is growing.

- **Goal Setting**: Goal setting can be a great way to clarify your focus, measure progress, and track achievements. Goals are essential as they can help keep a business on track. Creating a business plan or even single targeted tasks can help your business reach new levels of success, but keep in mind that there is a large difference between realistic and achievable goals. Your goals should be specific, measurable, realistic, timely, and attainable. The starting point for setting in place realistic goals is communication, especially from those at the leadership level. Communication should be prioritized not only internally, but externally as well.

- **Delegate**: Small business owners often find themselves taking on every task in their company, but as a business grows, this hands-on approach becomes harder to maintain. The evolution of a business depends on its leader's ability to let go of that death grip and learn to delegate without micromanaging. It is not easy but necessary to delegate so you can focus on keeping your business growing. Here are some ways to make delegation a little easier:
  - Start by recording everything you do in a week and then consider which tasks don't require your level of skill and expertise, such as administrative or sales.
  - Choose the right person to delegate the task to, and the right person will depend on the task you are delegating; for example, ask yourself if that person has the ability to either learn or has the skill set to take on that particular task. If the answer is yes, then provide support; if the answer is no, then hire a professional who can do the task without your management.
  - It's important to build feedback into the delegation process, both yours and the person you chose to delegate tasks to, which will always keep both of you on the same page and you'll feel better knowing the task is being performed correctly.

- **Continuous Learning**: Staying competitive in today's global marketplace means that companies need to be innovative, adaptive, and ever-changing. You need to learn new knowledge or skills in order to see things in a new light and take that next leap. When businesses do not support a continual process of learning, innovation does not happen, processes remain unchanged, and nothing new is ever accomplished. Management, as well as employees, need to challenge themselves in order to obtain new knowledge, ideas, and skills. Learning needs to be on a flexible, on-demand, and on a continual basis in order to contribute this kind of cutting-edge performance. Creating a learning culture within the company is an effective way to improve performance and innovation, but also employees' satisfaction and retention. As the saying goes, "knowledge is power" and this could not be more important to a business that wants to grow to the next level. No matter how much you achieve, there will always be more you can learn and apply for even greater success.

Should I Continue to Protect the Brand of My Growing Business?

Focused on taking their business to the next level, many business owners overlook one important thing: continuing to protect the business brand as the business achieves higher levels of success. Brands today are generally recognized as a key asset creating value for your business. So why are business owners still paying so little attention to developing brand value for their growing business?

Trademarking your business name at the launch of your company isn't an umbrella to protect future logos, product names, marketing slogans, and other branding assets. Each brand asset needs its own trademark registration. As your business grows, so should protection of your brand. Developing a brand image should not be your last priority to be addressed only after your business is established.

Your brand image should be developed in parallel with your business, and the branding strategy should constitute an integral part of your business plan. What is the use of making major investments into developing quality products and services if that quality reputation cannot be captured and developed in the form of your brand image? It is through your brand image that your business will attract and retain loyal customers for your products and services.

Continuing to develop your brand image requires time, effort, and commitment, and certainly some financial resources, but not as much as you might expect. It is a wise investment to make for your company.

Key Takeaways

- Growing your company takes money and where to look for it takes time. There are two ways to externally fund a business: debt and equity. Do your homework on which type of funding you are willing to take on, as both have their advantages and disadvantages. Knowing where to find the money is half the struggle of growing your business.
- Those who have survived Startup and are successfully managing your growing business may be wondering how to take the next step and grow the business beyond its current status. Like it or not, your business expenses

go up each year, and to stay profitable, your business needs to grow so it can absorb those increases. Decide on which strategy or strategies will be best for your business and will help keep more of your money in your pocket as you grow.

- Trademarking your business name at the launch of your company isn't an umbrella to protect future logos, product names, marketing slogans, and other branding assets. Each brand asset needs its own trademark registration. As your business grows, so should protection of your brand. Developing a brand image should not be your last priority to be addressed only after your business is established.

A STORY OF CAUTION FOR GROWTH COMPANIES

Growing Without a Plan

There are many stories about businesses failing and many reasons for those failures. But one of the main reasons that businesses fail in the Growth phase is due to unplanned rapid growth.

My clients had a car-detailing business, and they were the best at what they did. They used environmentally friendly products, so they charged a little more, and they serviced their customers' cars from a shop they rented. As time went by, they realized that more and more people were using their services because of the environmentally friendly products. As demand rose, so did their rent. Instead of renegotiating their lease with the landlord or looking for a new shop to rent, they decided to obtain a loan and buy their own real property to house their shop.

Within a few months of buying their own real property, they decided they wanted to reach customers outside their local community and implemented mobile car-detailing services. They had to drive to the customer's location, so they charged more on top of their already high prices. For the mobile car-detailing service, they needed to hire employees. Without running the numbers, they hired 15 employees to drive to customer locations and provide mobile services. My clients failed to realize that some markets are just not profitable. You can spend time, energy, and lots of money reaching them, but some markets are not willing to pay top dollar for particular services.

Within eight months of buying a new property and hiring 15 employees, they came to the realization that they could no longer pay all their expenses and still stay in business. They lost the new shop, they laid off all the employees, and were forced to start over again.

Why waste so much of your time and money reaching a customer base that doesn't have the need or the means to buy your product or service? It would have made much more sense for my clients to stay small and serve the customers who were happy and willing to pay for their services rather than growing too fast without a plan.

Growing a business, you have nurtured from the beginning can be exciting. However, just because you have succeeded in entering the Growth phase does not mean your business will sustain the growth. It is important to be aware of the common mistakes that can occur during the growth phase and hinder your growth. Here are the three most common mistakes I see business owners make while growing their company and ways to overcome them:

1. **Not defining the company's mission, vision, and values.**
   It sounds simple, but having a clearly defined mission, vision, and set of values can help achieve alignment in your company.

(Continued)

- The mission statement is the core of your company's purpose: what the company does, and what the desired outcome is.
- The vision of the company should keep you and your employees motivated. It is the business owner's role to create the vision of where the company is going and share that vision with the employees to make sure everyone understands where the company is headed.
- Values are the principles and behaviors that describe how the company does business and what impression you want your customers to have.

2. **Not understanding the roles and responsibilities of the business owner**.

   Too many business owners think their job is to make all the decisions and be at the center of everything. The fact is that too many business owners find themselves working "in the business" rather than "on the business." You need to understand how your roles and responsibilities change during the various stages of growth and how your behavior affects the company's overall growth. It is very important for the business owner to delegate, communicate effectively, and plan ahead so the owner doesn't become the obstacle to the growth of the company.

3. **Relying on luck**.

   Some companies are in the right place at the right time and experience growth because the economy was growing, the owner had good networks, and business came easily without having to do much work. If you are going to keep your business moving up the growth curve, you need to be prepared for a market change and have a growth strategy that targets various customers. You need to plan for the future and develop the infrastructure to support growth.

My husband is a Marine and one thing he learned during his time in the Corp was: "Proper prior planning prevents piss poor performance." Words every business owner should live by.

PART 3

Established Phase

I've missed more than 9,000 shots in my career. I've lost almost 300 games. Twenty-six times I've been trusted to take the game-winning shot and missed. I've failed over and over and over again in my life, and that is why I succeed.

– Michael Jordan

The Knight represents the professional soldier whose job it is to protect those of rank. The Established phase represents your company as being stable and known to customers as a recognized brand.

CHAPTER 7

How Does My Business Stay Competitive?

A business goes through stages of development similar to the human cycle of life. Parenting strategies that work for your toddler cannot be applied to your teenager. The same goes for your business, which will face different cycles throughout its life. What you focus on today will change and require different approaches to maintain success. This brings us to the Established phase of your business. Let's first define what established is in the business world.

What Is Established?

There are many ways to define an established business, but the one that really resonates is when your business has matured into a thriving company with a place in the market and loyal customers. An established business is one that has obtained a reputation for a specific product, service, process, or platform. Most established companies will aim to continue to grow and develop their customer base within their particular industry.

In the Established phase, sales growth is not explosive but manageable, and business life has become more routine. An established business will be focused on improvement and productivity. To compete in an established market, you will need better business practices along with automation and outsourcing to improve productivity.

I have found that when business owners reach this phase, the planning is about making decisions today based on your assessment of likely future events. It is also about trying to minimize risks. The number one question most frequently asked in the Established phase is how a business stays competitive.

How Does My Business Stay Competitive?

Companies remain competitive through the use of well-planned strategies. Being a competitor requires constant monitoring of your company and the events that are taking place around you. To remain profitable, a company must have strategies available that it employs to stay competitive in the marketplace. To reach company goals, a business must employ strategic planning that identifies potential problems, creates the framework to help develop a budget, and recommends the effective use of company personnel as a road map to achieving business goals. A company cannot remain competitive if it does not take the time to analyze the path ahead and create a plan to avoid the problems and benefit from the opportunities.

There are three main areas of a business that help keep the company competitive and strategies must be planned around these. The three main areas are pricing, first to market, and personnel.

- **Pricing**: Pricing may not always be the top reason why customers use a particular product, but the cost of a product to the consumer needs to remain fair for the consumer to justify the purchase. Unless you are one of the Louis Vuittons of the world, pricing will be a factor for consumers. Developing competitive pricing requires strategies that involve proper personnel forecasting, purchase costs of raw materials, and shipping costs to the distributor. A company must maintain the lowest production costs possible to offer competitive pricing in the marketplace.
- **First to Market**: Product and technology innovation are important to a company that is looking to stay competitive. Being first to market with innovative and high-quality products helps a company develop a reputation as a market leader. When a company is recognized as a market leader, it helps increase effectiveness of marketing and increases the return on the advertising dollars spent. When a company is consistently first to market, it can dictate the competitive playing field of its industry and remain a top competitor.
- **Personnel**: Top companies are constantly searching for the best talent in their industry. A proactive headhunter company will have a list of available candidates for positions within your industry who have the exact experience you are looking for. When a company is growing, it remains competitive by identifying its future personnel needs and acquiring the talent to meet personnel demands.

Businesses compete for customers. Ultimately, the success of a business depends on its ability to attract and keep customers. Asking how your business will compete is one of the simplest yet most important questions you can ask. It's one of the questions you need to answer when writing your business plan, both in the Startup phase and once when your business is growing and enters the Established phase. There are thousands of articles that have been written over the years that provide advice on how to stay competitive. After talking to my successful clients, I have compiled the top strategies used by them to stay competitive in their respective industries. Here is a list of proven strategies:

- **Know your Competition**: Competitive analysis has become an essential part of business marketing activity and has made it possible to perform strategic planning. While analyzing your competitors, you should know what you are looking for and how it can help your business. It is not about stealing your competitor's ideas. It's about revealing their strengths and weaknesses and finding your own company's competitive advantages. So how do you go about finding your competitors? Here are some ways that have worked very well for my clients:
  - **Attend Professional Conferences**: Attending professional conferences and trade shows is a great way to learn about who your competitors are and what they offer.
  - **Analyze Industry Reports**: Companies that are publicly held will file reports with the U.S. Securities Exchange Commission. These reports will reveal a lot of information about your competitors' business regarding new products.
  - **Analyze Websites**: By visiting the websites of your competitors, you'll learn a lot about how they market their products or services and what types of deals they offer for first time buyers or existing buyers.
- **Know your Customers**: For businesses to be profitable they need a clear understanding of who their customers are and what drives them to buy. Getting insights into the minds of customers is extremely difficult. But it is possible to improve customer experience by leveraging information that is acquired by implementing the right processes. Here are a few ways of getting to know your customer better:
  - **Leverage Social Media**: Having a social media account is a must for businesses that can leverage it to interact with their customers. Social media platforms provide insights on customer habits and most importantly what they are buying. You can use this platform to interact with potential customers and ask them directly what they like, what they don't like, and what they are willing to pay for your product or service.
  - **Conduct Surveys**: Surveys are one of the best methods to gain honest feedback from customers regarding a product or service, which provides

you information on what your customers are thinking and how they feel about your product or service.

- **Conduct Keyword Research**: The mindset of your customer is better understood by using the keywords that they use to search for your product or service. Customers conduct vigorous online research for the items they want to purchase and most importantly, from whom they want to purchase. Keyword research allows you to understand the interests of your target markets and the terms that customers use to find the products or services they want.

- **Know your SWOT**: The acronym SWOT stands for Strengths, Weaknesses, Opportunities, and Threats. A SWOT analysis is one of the most important strategic tools available to a company, as it provides a great way for you to examine both positive and negative attributes that determine how best to compete in the marketplace. SWOT analysis is an in-depth look at exactly how a company operates. It examines the strengths of the company, acknowledges its weak points, and identifies both opportunities and threats. These are all useful pieces of information that in most cases will help a company succeed. In conducting a SWOT analysis, a company evaluates its current position in the market and compares it to the future opportunities and risks that could affect it moving forward.

What really makes SWOT powerful is its usefulness in setting a course to take advantage of prime business opportunities. Without a strategic plan, companies can just aimlessly drift around without a strategic direction, or operate without development. In highly competitive industries, failing to seize openings is almost as catastrophic as making a major mistake. If a new customer segment emerges due to shifts in preferences, for instance, it is often a race to see which company best serves the need first. SWOT allows you to map out this possible opportunity well in advance, and begin planning to deliver a quality solution and marketing plan before the opening hits.

Though it is not always pleasant to scrutinize your weaknesses or deficiencies, top companies know where they stand in all critical areas relative to the competition. Walmart is renowned for its low prices in discount retail, for example, but company leaders likely recognize criticism of its limited customer services. With some weaknesses, you have opportunities to improve. With strategic limitations tied to its low-price strategy, the goal of Walmart is more to downplay the weakness, target customers who prefer low prices, and promote that core benefit.

Threats are another key SWOT element in guarding against risks. Companies that don't use a planning tool like SWOT may be caught off guard when threats emerge. In contrast, effective use of SWOT helps a business adjust or prepare for pending threats. Some businesses wait until a recession slows revenue, for instance, while others recognize the potential for recession in advance and alter their strategies and trim their budgets.

- **Know Your Partnerships**: Business partnerships connect you with existing companies that have the tools and audience to help you grow. These organizations have spent years building their reputation and aligning yourself with them in a smart way will enable you to tap into their reputation and create credibility within the industry. Working with the right partners can have a tremendous impact on your overall growth. Here are some top advantages to finding strategic partners and using them to market your business:
  - **New Audiences**: Companies spend years growing an audience through content distribution and advertising and gradually build a strong list of interested customers and prospects. Through your partnership, you'll have a unique opportunity to tap into these audiences and reach a new pool of customers. By working with a company closely aligned with what you sell, you can reach a highly targeted group of individuals. When your partner promotes your brand, you instantly earn the trust of the existing audience, making it easier to grow your own base of prospects and customers.
  - **Better Competition**: Every business has competition; however, to compete with your competition and attract a larger share of the market, partnerships can help. You can get more exposure, offer better deals than your competitors, and position your business more strategically in the marketplace.
  - **Social Good**: Partnering with non-profit organizations or causes specific to your core value can also have a tremendous impact on your business growth. Customers love to see companies give back, and sponsoring a local charity event or giving a portion of every sale to the non-profit can help with attracting new customers.
- **Become an Expert**: To truly beat your competition and separate yourself from the pack, you need to position your business as an expert in its field. Becoming a recognized expert is a process in which you must adopt a proactive approach. Here are a few ways you can establish yourself and your business as a leader in your field:
  - **Write a Book about Your Industry**: One of the quickest ways to obtain instant credibility is to author a book. What do people need to know about your industry? What helpful advice can you offer? Can you teach someone how to do something? It's about making their lives better by sharing valuable information.
  - **Write about Your Industry**: Look for opportunities to author articles about your industry and provide articles or news items to publications

and trade magazines within your industry. Editors are always looking for interesting and informative content, so offer your expert advice. Your name will not only appear under the title as the author, you most likely will have an author's bio at the end of the piece, where you can provide your contact information, website, and social media addresses.

- **Get Involved in Your Industry**: Become a member of the leading association related to your industry and possibly join the board of directors, volunteer, speak at, and sponsor various events. You'll engage with other notables from whom you can learn and you'll establish yourself in a leadership position.

- **Create an Online Presence**: It is actually expected in today's business world that you use your website and social media outlets to create a strong and authoritative online presence. Use Twitter to send out updates or links to helpful articles, build a following on LinkedIn, and promote your speaking engagements. Think of what you know that can benefit other people then develop ways to disseminate that information through all the technologies and methods available today.

- **Keep Innovating**: In today's world, it is crucial to stay on the cutting edge of your industry. By constantly innovating, you will stay focused on the goal while keeping your customers interested in your company. Older companies are great to look to for leadership in innovation. How have they managed to keep up with the times? What company policies allow them to continue to innovate and change while functioning well for their customer base? These questions will help you see the logic of innovation.

How Do I Stay Focused?

It happens all the time. Many business owners become scattered and distracted in both strategy and execution, trying to move in too many directions at the same time. This lack of focus ends up causing a lack of real movement for your business in any one particular direction and can ultimately lead to failure.

More than likely, you understand that focus is important as you have probably been told that most of your life. However, when companies enter the Established phase, they tend to forget about focus. After all, what could go wrong since you made it this far? The problem is that a lack of focus leads to scattered resources. Devoting time, energy, and money to multiple strategies and marketing channels at the same time leads to none of them being executed well. All of this in turn leads to frustration, lack of progress for the business, and ultimately failure.

To achieve extreme focus for your business there are three major areas to consider: the overall strategy for your business, campaigns for achieving your overall strategy, and finally the daily activities and tasks associated with execution. The overall strategy is the big picture and the ultimate direction as well as purpose of the business. This is usually something that does not change unless you are making a major market shift and pivoting. Within the overall strategy you should focus on your unique value proposition – the value your company promises to deliver to customers. Campaigns and initiatives support your overall strategy and you should focus on one marketing channel at a time. One of the biggest faults of being unfocused in your marketing is never giving each marketing channel a fair shot by not dedicating enough time, energy, or money, and giving up too early. Finally, your daily and weekly focus will include tactics and activities that fall in line with achieving your campaigns, as well as your overall strategy.

Why Is a Business Plan Important?

You may have heard about business plans and paid no attention. After all, who has time to sit and write one? Take another look at the concept of a business plan. What is a business plan? In its simplest form, a business plan is a guide, a road map for your business that outlines your goals and details how you plan to achieve those goals. A well-written business plan is an important tool because it gives business owners the ability to lay out their goals and track their progress as their business begins to grow and change. Formulating a business plan should be the first thing you do when starting your business, but the beauty of business plans is that you can create one anytime during your Business Legal Lifecycle®.

Business plans typically include detailed information that can help improve the chances of success for your business. While business plans have many purposes, the primary importance of a business plan is that it helps business owners make better decisions. Entrepreneurship is often an endless exercise in decision-making and crisis management. Sitting down and considering all the ramifications of any given decision is a luxury that entrepreneurs cannot always afford. That's where the business plan comes in. Building a business plan allows you to determine the answer to some of the most critical business decisions ahead of time, such as your marketing strategy and your selling propositions. You'll answer many tough questions before they arise. Here are some very important reasons a business plan can help your company:

- **Map the Future**: A business plan is a vital tool to help you manage your business more effectively. By committing your thoughts to paper, you can understand your business better and set specific courses of action needed to improve your business. A plan can detail alternative future scenarios, set specific objectives and goals, and include the resources required to achieve these goals.
- **Develop and Communicate a Course of Action**: A business plan helps your company assess future opportunities and commit to a particular course of action. The plan can assign milestones to specific individuals and, ultimately, help management monitor progress.
- **Support Growth and Secure Funding**: Most businesses face investment decisions during the course of their lifetime. Often you can't fund these opportunities on your own and must seek funding elsewhere. Any investor who is interested in funding your business must have an excellent understanding of where the company is planning to go and what the company plans to do with the funding. Therefore, when seeking investment for your business, it is important to clearly describe the opportunity for potential investors. A well-written business plan can help you convey to the investor your company's future ability to generate sufficient cash flow to meet debt obligation, while enabling the business to operate effectively.
- **Help Manage Cash Flow**: Careful management of cash flow is a fundamental requirement for all businesses. The reason is quite simple: Many businesses fail, not because they are not profitable, but because they cannot pay their debts when due, which could be prevented by managing cash flow.
- **Support a Strategic Exit**: Finally, at some point, you will decide it is time to exit your company. If you consider your likely exit strategy in advance and the different ways you can sell your business, the plan will help you direct present-day decisions. You can make investment decisions now while keeping one eye on the future via a well-thought-out business plan.

A good business plan follows generally accepted guidelines for both form and content. There are three primary parts to a business plan. The first is the business concept, where you discuss the industry, your business structure, your particular products or services, and how you plan to make your business a success. The second is your target market in which you describe and analyze potential customers as to who they are, where they are, and what makes them buy your products or services. You will also describe the competition and how you'll position yourself to beat it. Finally, there's the financial section, which contains your income and cash flow statements, balance sheet, and other financial ratios, such as breakeven analyses.

Some business plans will run 5 or 8 pages, while others will be 80-plus pages. The complexity of the business and details necessary to present a thorough picture of the business will define the appropriate length of your business plan. Regardless of the length of the plan, the three primary parts of the business plan are further broken down into these key elements:

- **Executive Summary**: The executive summary provides an overview of the rest of the business plan. It is often considered the most crucial part of the plan because it is the first section your readers see and is designed to capture their attention. The executive summary should include:
  - Overall objective of the business, such as what makes the business unique or distinctive
  - Experience of your management team and who they are
  - Target audience and where to find them
  - Future aspirations
  - How the business will operate
  - Current competition in the market
  - Costs and financial projections
- **Company Description or Business Overview**: This section is used to explain your vision and goals for the business venture in practical terms. The who, what, when, where, and why of the business should fall into place, and readers should have a clear understanding of how the company will function. Details that prospective investors and management team members will likely want to see are:
  - Legal structure of the business
  - Formation of the business
  - Type of business
  - Potential for profitability
  - Geographical location of the business
  - Means of doing business
  - Resources required
- **Products or Services**: This section describes the products sold or services offered. Explain the significant benefits of your products or services and how they provide something other than that which is currently available.
- **Market Information**: Market information describes the larger picture of the industry in which your business will compete. This sets a framework so that investors will see what piece of this market you will be able to capture and from where you will build your customer base. It also provides you with an opportunity to carefully research and evaluate the industry to better determine how you can make an impact. Market information must

be timely, accurate, and easy to understand. Furthermore, you should present:
- An overview of the market
- Trends and changes in the market
- Niche markets and segments within the larger market
- Your target audience
- The needs of your target audience
- How you will impact those needs
- How you anticipate the market will change over the next five years

- **Competitive Analysis**: Business is competitive by nature, and to succeed it is vital that you research, understand, and evaluate your competition. The strengths, weaknesses, and details of the most direct and indirect competition should be included in this section of your business plan.
- **Management and Ownership**: You may have heard the saying, "It's the team behind the company that people invest in," so this section should highlight and feature short biographies of the key personnel involved in forming and running the business. Explaining who is behind the company and what each person brings to the table is of great interest to any potential investor.
- **Financial Plan**: from startup costs to the day-to-day operational budget, a solid financial plan should be outlined within the overall business plan. The financial section should outline:
  - How much money is necessary to start the business?
  - How much money will be needed over the next two to five years?
  - How will funds be used?
  - A timeline of when you will need funding

Business plans tend to have a lot of elements in common, like cash flow projections and marketing plans, and many of them share certain objectives as well, such as raising money or setting goals for the future. But business plans are not all the same any more than all businesses are. Depending on your business and what you intend to use your plan for, you may need a very different type of business plan from another entrepreneur. Plans differ widely in their length, their appearance, the detail of their contents, and the varying emphases they place on different aspects of the business. In your Established phase, you'll most likely focus on setting short-term goals and laying out milestones to achieve those goals, which will keep you on your toes and on the cutting edge of your industry. Business plans are a living document and will change with time as your company changes and grows; your business plan should be reviewed regularly and updated as required.

For a business plan template please visit: www.wiley.com/go/bagla/golegalyourself. (Password: Bagla123).

Key Takeaways

- Companies remain competitive through the use of well-planned strategies. Being a competitor requires constant monitoring of your company and the events that are taking place around you. To remain profitable, a company must have strategies available that it employs to stay competitive in the marketplace.
- When companies enter the Established phase, they tend to forget about focus. After all, what could go wrong, since you made it this far? The problem is that a lack of focus leads to scattered resources. Devoting time, energy, and money to multiple strategies and marketing channels at the same time leads to none of them being executed well.
- A business plan is a guide, a road map for your business that outlines your goals and details how you plan to achieve those goals. A well-written business plan is an important tool because it gives business owners the ability to lay out their goals and track their progress as their business begins to grow and change. Formulating a business plan should be the first thing you should do when starting your business, but the beauty of business plans is that you can create one anytime during your Business Legal Lifecycle®.

CHAPTER 8

How Do I Enter New Markets?

Many companies dream of expanding their business into new markets, which can be an effective way to leverage your established reputation. Once a business is established and thriving in its home market, it is often seen as the right time to branch out into a new market. If a company enjoys strong sales, has great brand awareness, and the business is stable overall, it may be the right time to take the plunge.

I have helped some of my clients who were in the Established phase evolve by entering into new markets, buying out their competition, or merging with strategic partners, allowing them to retain their competitive edge. The second most frequently asked question in the Established phase is how to enter new markets.

How Do I Enter New Markets?

At this stage, I'm assuming you have established your business within your industry and now are looking to expand your market. Just because you are a small business does not mean you should not be thinking big. Business owners usually start doing business in their own state and then expand to other states. Sometimes it may make sense for the business to be ambitious and consider expanding globally.

Whether you are expanding nationwide or globally, it takes a disciplined process to accurately assess the new market. Investing in the appropriate level of resources in market analysis, market selection, and market entry method can create a foundation for success in the chosen market. But first a lot of research is required to gain a deep understanding of the targeted market, the competition, market trends, and the requirements to successfully launch and drive your business into that market.

Before taking action and expanding, it is critical to understand what the full impact on your business will be. The following process will provide you with a technique for properly assessing the opportunities and risks of a new market:

- **Define the Market**: Clearly defining your market may seem like a simple step but before you identify who you want to sell your products or services to, it is important to understand the new consumer needs. You will need to consider the demographics, location, and common interests or needs of your target customers. Try to answer these questions:
  - Who are your potential customers?
  - Where do they live?
  - Do they have common interests or habits?
  - Do you have access to buyer personas?
- **Perform Market Analysis**: Expanding into new markets involves a great deal of market research. Prepare a market segmentation analysis to determine if your products or services will sell in that market. You will need to develop an in-depth understanding of that market, its demands, its competition, and potential barriers to entry. Try to answer these questions:
  - Who are your competitors within that market?
  - Are there any barriers to entering that market?
  - How quickly is the market growing?
  - What is the forecasted demand for your products or services?
- **Access Internal Capabilities**: Much of your decision on how to enter a new market is driven by your internal capabilities and the available resources you can deploy for such expansion. Introducing a new plan when your internal team is not ready or cannot meet the deadlines will end up being a disappointment for everyone. Try to answer these questions:
  - How do you ready your staff for new challenges?
  - What difficulties, if any, will be placed on your team?
  - What resources do you need to enter new markets?
  - What financial capacity will you require?
- **Define Market Entry**: Develop a strategy and business plan, as each market has its own nuances due to economic, cultural, governmental, and market conditions. It is important to develop a strategy and business plan that drives success in the new markets while remaining integrated with the overall company strategy and objectives. Establish a strong team, as many companies try to launch their expansion with a team put together rapidly

from scratch. This is time-consuming, risky, and slows time to market. Using proven senior team members allows the company to hit the ground running, while the company hires the right senior management team to take over the new markets. It is important to establish a go-to-market strategy, as effective selling and marketing of your products or services requires a comprehensive strategy that addresses sales delivery, branding, marketing, and pricing. It's extremely important that you be in legal readiness, as some states and countries are known for being highly litigious, so it is critical to put strong legal processes in place to minimize risk. Also, government agencies have strict requirements that necessitate legal documentation be in place prior to operating within the state or country. Being proactive does require money up front, but this more than offsets downstream risks and liabilities. Here are some proactive actions to consider:

- Create localized commercial agreements addressing dispute resolution
- Review industry-specific regulations to ensure that compliance and certifications are obtained if needed
- Maintain corporate records and governance

You will also be required to be in tax and financial readiness, as the proper tax and financial infrastructures need to be set up early on to ensure that you can take full advantage of the tax benefits available to your business. Here are some actions to take:

- Set up accounting and payroll
- Establish local banking relationships
- Develop a risk-management plan with your CPA

Exploring the various market entry strategies can help you better understand which strategies best fit your business. Here are some common strategies used for market entry:

- Direct selling – selling products or services directly to the consumer
- Exporting – producing your goods in your home country and selling them abroad
- Licensing – providing authorization to another company to sell your goods on your behalf
- Franchising – granting another company the right to use your business model in return for royalties
- Partnering – establishing a long-term relationship with a trusted source to sell your goods
- Joint ventures – establishing a relationship with another company to pool your resources together

Here are some additional questions you should consider answering before entering a new market:

- Will your products or services sell well in the targeted market? The good news is that most American products and services are embraced both nationally and overseas.
- Is your target market familiar with your products or services? If not, be prepared to invest a lot of time and money in consumer education. On the flip side, if you are the first one to introduce a new and exciting concept, the product then becomes synonymous with your company name.
- Do you feel comfortable doing business in that state or country? Since you might have to live there temporarily to operate the business in its early stages, you will need a working knowledge of the way business is done in that state or country.

What Business Laws Should I Know?

Once you have decided to enter into a new market, be it in another state or another country, it's highly recommended that you research any restrictions and regulations that may affect you when selling your goods. Here are some business laws that you should pay close attention to, as they can become very costly if ignored:

- **Taxes**: Every state and country has different expectations and standards when it comes to taxes. For instance, if your company's demographic is located in the U.S., you'll likely want to display your prices exclusive of tax. However, if your target market is in England, where shoppers are accustomed to seeing all-inclusive prices, you'll want to include tax. To cover all your bases, talk to a tax professional as this expert will be able to help you understand specific circumstances that may affect your business by providing you with insights on how you need to charge tax.
- **Payment Gateways**: There are many payment gateways available for businesses. When you're vetting payment gateways, be sure to ask if they have any limitations around certain products, as well as whether they are hosted or non-hosted, whether they include anti-fraud features or require transaction fees, termination fees, monthly fees, or setup fees. The most commonly used payment gateways include:
  - PayPal
  - Square
  - Stipe
  - First Data
  - QuickBooks Online
  - SecureNet

- **Patents and Trademarks**: As you enter new territories, you should definitely check with the local patent and trademark organization to make sure you are not infringing on other patents or trademarks with your products or services.

As a business owner who wants to take your business to the next level, it pays to do your homework. Start early and strategize as to where you foresee your business going, as not every business is suited for such expansion.

Key Takeaways

- Whether you are expanding nationwide or globally, it takes a disciplined process to accurately assess the new market. Investing the appropriate level of resources in market analysis, market selection, and market entry method can create a foundation for success in the chosen market. But first a lot of research is required to gain a deep understanding of the targeted market, the competition, market trends, and the requirements to successfully launch and drive your business into that market.
- Before taking action and expanding, it is critical to understand what the full impact on your business will be. Implement the process to help avoid mistakes that could cost you a lot of money.
- Once you have decided to enter into a new market, be it in another state or another country, it's highly recommended that you research any restrictions and regulations that may affect you when selling your goods.

CHAPTER 9

How Do I Retain Good People?

Retaining key employees is critical to the long-term health and success of your business. While it's not easy to find good employees, it's even more difficult keeping them motivated and inspired to work hard. Many jobs become routine for employees, who eventually seek greener pastures elsewhere.

In the Established phase, employee turnover should not be as high as it might have been in earlier stages. By now you should have created a company culture where employees want to work, grow with the company, and stay. The third most frequently asked question in the Established phase how to retain good people.

How Do I Retain Good People?

According to strategic planning consultant Leigh Branham, author of *The 7 Hidden Reasons Employees Leave*, 88% of employees leave their jobs for reasons other than pay. However, 70% of managers think employees leave mainly for pay-related reasons. Here are Branham's seven reasons employees leave a company:

1. Employees feel the job or workplace is not what they expected.
2. There is a mismatch between the job and person.
3. There is too little coaching and feedback.
4. There are too few growth and advancement opportunities.
5. Employees feel devalued and unrecognized.
6. Employees feel stress from overwork and have a work/life imbalance.
7. There is a loss of trust and confidence in senior leaders.

After you put in the time, effort, and investment to hire the best employees possible, your goal should be to retain that talent. Salary, retirement plans, and vacation benefits are high on the list of why employees take the job, but they are not enough to keep them in your employ for the long haul. So, how can you keep your best talent? Here are a few strategies you can use to retain your top talent:

- **Hire the Right People:** It all begins with hiring the right person for the right position. Each job position should have a comprehensive description and that description should be updated frequently. Those doing the hiring will need to assess job candidates thoroughly and make sure they have the skills and personality to cope with the job and fit in with the culture of your company.

- **Create a Great Work Environment:** A work environment that makes people feel included will encourage employees to stay. Create an environment that makes your employees feel like an asset to your company and a place where they will enjoy spending time. Offer free coffee and snacks and maybe provide a pool table or other light games where they can take a break and wind down. Celebrate birthdays, throw parties as a reward for completion of successful projects, and have happy hour on a Friday, which can all help create a positive working environment.

- **Value Your Employees:** There are many small ways to show that you value your employees. Just acknowledging their contribution and saying "thank you" can make a big difference. Small perks such as free meals, free parking, and flexible scheduling all help to increase morale. Rewards for a job well done may come in various forms, such as a bonus check or a gift certificate to a nice restaurant. Recognition needs to be specific. What's more, don't hesitate to mention projects employees are working on so they know you are engaged with what they are doing. In order to retain talent, you must make them feel appreciated, respected, and worthwhile. They need to feel that their contributions to the company are important. Allow them to feel secure in their job and acknowledge their contributions to the company. Get their input about your company, and encourage goal setting so they feel a sense of accomplishment once the goals are achieved.

- **Provide Opportunities:** If employees feel they cannot see a future within the company, they will look for better opportunities elsewhere. If you enable them to acquire more skills and progress in their careers, they are far more likely to remain loyal. Provide opportunities to grow and learn, and let your employees know there is room for advancement in your company. Provide tuition for continuing education classes, which shows that you really care about providing opportunities for advancement. Give them challenging and stimulating work. Let them know what career-development plans you have for them and what opportunities are available for them to grow with the company.

- **Offer Competitive Benefits:** Companies that offer the most benefits to their employees are more likely to keep them. Many surveys reveal that health benefits are most important, followed by retirement funds. With the costs of healthcare rising, a strong employee health benefit plan is essential to recruit top talent. Creating a retirement plan for your employees where you offer a 401(k) match could be very attractive for longevity and be a great motivator for staying on with your company.
- **Prioritize Work–Life Balance:** Work–life balance has become more important to employees than ever before. You need to acknowledge that your employees have a life outside of work. If you consistently make them come in early and work after hours, they will inevitably start looking for other jobs. With the ability to work remotely, it has become easier for people to work without having to go into the office. Working remotely offers the kind of flexibility that employees want and are looking for.
- **Establish Open Communication:** Many bosses don't realize the importance of communicating with employees and making them feel connected. Employees often experience a lack of feedback; they don't know how they are doing and that could make them feel uncomfortable. It helps to periodically conduct interviews with employees to find out how things are going. When you listen to them, it shows you value them.

What Types of Employee Agreements and Policies Do I Need?

Good retention starts from the time you hire employees to the time they leave your company. I have seen business owners lose their top people to their customers or other companies, which usually leaves the business owner devastated due to the loss of such great talent. This happens more often than you think. Without safeguarding your investment, your top talent, you have just lost a lot of money. Top employees are not created overnight; you put a lot of money, time, and effort into training them, and losing them to another company could be disastrous for yours. Moreover, now you need to find someone else just as talented and put more money, time, and effort into training this new person. All the while, you are losing money from projects your top employee could have been working on.

At this stage of your company, you should have certain internal employee agreements, policies, and procedures that can safeguard such a loss — losing your top talent — at the same time protecting your legal rights as an employer. Here are some key agreements and policies you should use with every new hire:

- **Employee Agreement**: An employee agreement is a document used in relationships between employee and employer for the purpose of laying out the rights, responsibilities, and obligations of both parties during the employment period. Every employment agreement must contain the following terms:
  - **Job Information:** Some key pieces of information to start with include the job title, the job description, and to whom the employee reports.
  - **Compensation and Benefits:** Outline the compensation and benefits package to include the annual salary or hourly rate, information about raises, bonuses, or other incentives, and how they may be obtained.
  - **Time Off:** Time off includes sick days and vacation days, family emergencies, and any unpaid leave, which all need to be explained.
  - **Employee Classification:** Define whether the new hire is an employee or an independent contractor and spell out the treatment of their taxes. Many companies are facing lawsuits due to employment misclassification.
  - **Confidentiality:** Every company should protect its sensitive information, including trade secrets and client data, by including a confidentiality clause in the employee agreement.
  - **Termination:** Explain what is required for either party to terminate the relationship, including the amount of notice required and if it should be written notice, and any return of company property being used by the employee.
- **Employee Handbook**: An employee handbook is a document that contains your company's operating procedures and is used to establish important policies that are expected in the workplace and to protect the rights of both employer and employee. The handbook discloses legal information, such as the company's equal opportunity policy, workplace harassment policies, as well as expectations for safety in the workplace. An employee handbook has several advantages. It helps your company run more smoothly by outlining the dos and don'ts of the workplace. It encourages employee accountability and maintains stable job performance because the employee handbook makes it easy for the workers to understand what is expected of them. Employee handbooks also explain disciplinary procedures, which helps make performance management reviews more straightforward.

- **Employee Application Form**: An employee application form is used to gather information from job applicants during the hiring process. This form covers essential personal data and information to help make a hiring decision. A basic job application form should include the applicant's name, contact information, the position they are applying for, education, work history, and a place for them to sign and date. The importance of an employee application form is to hold all parties responsible for the information provided, in case a dispute later arises.
- **Invention Assignment Agreement**: An invention assignment agreement is a contract that gives the employer certain rights to inventions created by the employee during the employment relationship. This agreement is used by employers to safeguard the work that rightfully belongs to the company and not the individual employee. After all, as the employer, you are paying the employee to create work for the company.

What Are Other Ways to Retain Talent?

Many employers use various compensation methods to motivate and reward employees. These methods include issuance of stock, issuance of bonuses, and issuance of profit sharing. There are many benefits from offering these types of perks or incentives. For example, companies can save money by offering stock in lieu of cash payments, and employees become shareholders where they feel more invested in the company and willing to work harder to make their stock as valuable as possible. One of the most common methods of stock compensation is the stock option. A stock option is a contract that allows the holder to purchase a specified amount of stock at a specified price within a specified time period. The advantage is that even if the market value of the stock rises, the holder of the option may purchase the stock at the lower price set by the option contract. In order for a company to issue stock options, it must have a stock option plan, which is typically structured so that an employee must be employed by the company for a certain amount of time before he or she is able to exercise the option. Stock option plans still remain a valuable part of a long-term incentive package for employees who are expected to remain with the company for many years.

A monetary bonus can certainly serve as an incentive. However, it can also set a standard that may be hard to follow. Once word spreads that an employee received a monetary bonus, others will anticipate the same for their good work. Therefore, unless the bonus is part of an employment agreement, you need to establish a policy that details the expectations of an employee before he or she will be eligible to receive such a bonus. Besides cash bonuses, other types of incentive bonuses include gifts, extra vacation time, or extra personal days.

Another incentive offered by some companies is the profit-sharing plan. If a company is doing well, sharing profits with employees serves as a very strong incentive. Such plans will need to be carefully designed and spelled out with the assistance of professionals.

For all companies to thrive and become successful, they need to hire great talent and retain that talent. Employees should be valued and respected, and adopting the strategies above should give your company the advantage it needs.

Key Takeaways

- Top talent is hard to come by. After you put in the time, effort, and investment to hire the best employees possible, your goal should be to retain that talent. Salary, retirement plans, and vacation benefits are high on the list of why employees take the job, but they are not enough to keep them in your employ for the long haul.
- Good retention starts from the time you hire employees to the time they leave your company. I have seen business owners lose their top people to their customers or other companies, which usually leaves the business owner devastated due to the loss of such great talent. This happens more often than you think. Without safeguarding your investment, your top talent, you have just lost a lot of money.
- Many employers use various compensation methods to motivate and reward employees. These methods include issuance of stock, issuance of bonuses, and issuance of profit sharing.

A STORY OF CAUTION FOR ESTABLISHED COMPANIES

Losing Top Talent

Employees are free agents and can leave a job at any time for better pastures. Whether your company is large or small, having your best employee submit their notice can be trying. Great employees tend to take on a lot, which can leave you feeling alone, stressed, and betrayed when they inform you that they will be leaving. You may also have difficulty seeing how you will carry on after their departure. This happens all the time. The loss of great employees could be devastating for any company, both financially and emotionally.

One day, I received a phone call from a potential client. This company offered IT computer services and had just celebrated 10 years in business. The owner of the company grew his business from the ground up by hard work and by hiring ambitious people. He spent countless hours training and invested in additional resources in his employees.

The business owner shared with me that one of his top employees had just left, a person he had invested money, resources, and training into, and who had been with the company from the beginning. The employee managed all the top client accounts and had intimate knowledge of the workings of the business. The reason why the employee left the company was that the employee got a better offer from one of the business owner's clients. This sudden departure of a top employee came as a shock and, moreover, the business owner was left holding a list of unfinished projects and no extra hands to help. Instead of bringing in new business, he was forced to step in and work on the projects himself while at the same time looking for a replacement with equal skill. This sudden departure of his top employee cost the business owner close to $100,000 in lost business and time spent looking for and training new talent. Unfortunately, the loss of money could have been avoided by simply putting protective measures in place.

In order to minimize this type of loss in your business, you should have every employee contract stipulate language that if a customer of the company wants to hire any of the company's employees, then that customer would pay a hiring fee, which will cover the loss of revenue until you found a replacement employee. As a business owner, preparation is key, and being aware of some of the reasons that lead to the loss of a key employee is critical. We've already discussed some of the reasons employees leave, but here are some of the additional mistakes you should look out for and ways to avoid them:

- **Failure of Substandard Employee Contracts:** Employment law is complicated and employers usually get into a lot of legal trouble by not using attorney drafted employment agreements that have protective language in case things

(Continued)

don't work out. Having the right terminology in your employee contracts would save you thousands of dollars and lost time in replacing top employees. Always include a non-solicitation clause, which prevents the employees from seeking employment from your customers without your consent. In addition, always include language that will allow for such employment only on the basis of you receiving a fee from the customer to cover hiring new talent within a reasonable amount of time. This becomes a win-win situation whereby your employee is happy to work for your customer and you are happy with some financial compensation and can look for new talent without unexpected revenue loss.

- **Failure to Provide Vision:** Most employees do not get out of bed each morning trying to hit a profit number. They get out of bed to be a part of your company's vision and work toward achieving it. Successful business owners sell their employees a vision of the future and offer them an opportunity to be a part of that future. Include your employees in important goals you have for the company and ask for input as to how you can better achieve those goals. This gives the employees a sense of belonging and value.

- **Failure to Provide Guidance:** Almost every employee wants to have a discussion with you about his or her future with the company, and most business owners hardly engage with their employees about their careers with the company. Having that conversation with your top talent can provide a huge opportunity for your company, because if your best employees know there is a path for them going forward, they will be more likely to feel vested and stay on.

- **Failure to Provide Empathy:** Generally speaking, in today's workforce there is very little loyalty on either side. There is, however, a simple solution for this problem: Take the time to listen to your employees. The employee should leave the conversation believing you will take action on what was discussed. By leaving your door open to employee concerns and suggestions, you encourage them to feel they have a stake in the company; that you consider them important, and care enough to listen.

PART 4

Exit Phase

Disciplining yourself to do what you know is right and important, although difficult, is the high road to pride, self-esteem, and personal satisfaction.

– Margaret Thatcher

The King is the most important piece in the game. If your King is captured, you lose the game. The Exit phase is the most important phase in your Business Legal Lifecycle®, as this is the phase that sets you up for retirement or to start another venture. Without property planning and money, you can't do either.

CHAPTER 10

How Do I Exit My Business?

The process of selling a company can be one of the most emotionally taxing experiences a person can face. But with the right approach, it can also be one of the most rewarding. For many business owners, their business is their life's work. For others, their business is a primary source of income, one that has allowed them to live the life that they've worked hard to create. Whatever the result, a successful business must be protected because no business owner can work forever.

Ask most business owners about their exit strategy and you are likely to get blank stares. That's because the last thing on their mind is when and how they will retire from their business. Their focus is on being in the game or competing in their industry for as long as possible. Some owners understand the logic of planning for an exit, but typically put it off to some unknown point in the future.

This brings us to the fourth and final phase of your Business Legal Lifecycle®, the Exit phase. Let's first define what an exit from your business is.

What Is an Exit?

An exit from a business is when the business owner physically leaves their business permanently for whatever reason it may be. Generally, a strategic plan is put in place that describes and outlines the form that the departing transition will take. Just like you have written a business plan to guide your business throughout its Business Legal Lifecycle®, you should have one that guides it to a conclusion. Your business exit strategy does not have to mean disaster or failure, or even imminent action. In fact, many business owners start their business with the express purpose of exiting after a certain number of years. It does not mean they are less committed entrepreneurs; it just means they have a plan in place.

Selling a business can be the single most important decision of an entrepreneur's life, but it's more than just making the decision. Your business is typically the single largest asset you own, often with both real capital tied up and huge amounts of sweat equity invested. It's probably been the center of your life, where you have built relationships with partners, employees, and customers that are nearly like family. With all this at stake, few entrepreneurs ever plan their exit. Typically, they first begin to think about it when a prospective buyer approaches them, or worse, when external pressures like health, family, or partner problems force the issue.

Selling your business requires some forethought, strategizing, and careful implementation. In some ways, it is more complicated than starting a business. For instance, while there is really only one way to start a company, there are a handful of ways you can retire from your business.

The number one question most frequently asked in the Exit phase is how to exit a business.

How Do I Exit My Business?

Deciding to leave or sell the business you have worked so hard to grow is rarely an easy decision. As you think about your business exit strategy, you'll not only want to consider how you'll leave, but other factors that are involved with this process, such as will you make money when you exit your business? What will happen to your business after you leave? How long will your exit take? Far too often, business owners make assumptions about who will acquire their company and these beliefs tend to involve their children, key employees, or their competitors. However, if you aim to maximize the value of your business when you sell, you need to broaden your horizons as to who could be your buyer.

Your ideal buyer could very well be your competitor, or it could be a private equity firm seeking to purchase, grow, and resell your business years later for an increased return on investment. Or a firm aiming to incorporate your company's unique skills and expertise to bolster the growth of a platform company already on their books, so both companies evolve and develop together. Or it may be a professional buyer representing a firm in a completely different industry than yours, but with ambitions to diversify their services, perhaps sharing a culture similar to your company's.

Below are some examples of the different options, along with pros and cons, you have for a business exit:

- **Sell to Family**: You can sell your company to a family member. Many entrepreneurs want to keep their business in the family long term and that means making plans for transitioning the company to a child or another relative at a certain point. When you are considering selling your business, you may have possible buyers within your own family. You may want to withdraw from the business but still keep the business within the family. This may seem like an attractive business exit strategy because you can groom successors over time; just make sure your family relationships can handle the volatility and stress of business ownership. Although keeping the business in the family for multiple generations may seem like the best way to preserve your name in the business, it's important to be practical about who really is the best person for the job of running your business.

  The following are some positive reasons to choose this exit strategy:
  - You can choose and prepare the person you want to continue your business when you leave.
  - You are able to pass on your legacy.
  - You don't have to completely separate from your business and may be able to stay on in some sort of transitional or ongoing advisory role.

  The following are some negative reasons not to choose this exit strategy:
  - You may not find a family member who wants to, or is capable of, taking on the business.
  - This process may bring a lot of emotional, financial, and general stress to your family.
  - Employees, business partners, or investors may not support the individual in your family you choose.
- **Sell to Another Business**: You can sell your company to a private buyer. With a merger or acquisition business exit strategy, your company is either purchased by, or merges with, a company with similar or aligned goals to your business. This type of sale is usually conducted by buyers within your industry who are looking to buy similar businesses to enhance their current operations, products, or market presence. These buyers typically have resources to pay the highest value for your business because they have the greatest access to capital. Depending on who you merge with or sell your business to, this method could mean flexibility in terms of your involvement, or the freedom to walk away. Perhaps the best thing about this exit strategy is the ability to negotiate the price of the sale, but this process can take a long time.

The following are some positive reasons to choose this exit strategy:
- You'll be able to have a clean break from your business.
- You can negotiate the terms, price, and other details of the merger or acquisition.

The following are some negative reasons not to choose this exit strategy:
- This can be a time-consuming, costly, and perhaps even unsuccessful process.
- Your business may cease to exist as it once was with a range of possible consequences associated with this action.

- **Sell to Business Partner**: You can sell your company to your business partner. If there is more than one owner of a company, all the co-owners should have a buy–sell agreement between them that allows for one or more partners to buy out the selling partner. Usually, a buy–sell agreement will contain the terms of how the company will be valued and how the selling partner's interest will be bought out. This can be a very attractive offer to the selling partner and the remaining partners, as they will know the terms of the sale. This can be a business as usual exit strategy, depending on the buyer.

The following are some positive reasons to choose this exit strategy:
- Your business legacy will remain intact and for the most part, your business should continue to function as usual.
- You can exit your business fully and hopefully earn a profit on the sale of your share.
- You're dealing with a buyer you already know and work with, meaning the process should be much easier to approach.

The following are some negative reasons not to choose this exit strategy:
- Your business partner may not be willing to purchase your share.
- It may be more difficult to stay involved in your business in any capacity.
- The process could end up being contentious between you and your partner, leading to a range of potential problems.

- **Sell to Management**: You can sell your company to your management team. A management buyout involves the management team of a company combining resources to acquire all or part of your business. This allows for a smooth transition of ownership, and since the new owners know the company well, there is usually reduced risk of failure going forward. Although it may be difficult to plan ahead for many of these methods, it's possible that when you are ready to exit your business, people who already work for you may want to buy your company. As these individuals know you and know how to manage the company, this business exit strategy could result in a smoother transition and increase loyalty to your business legacy. Moreover, because these individuals are already part of your business and they likely know you so well, they may allow for flexibility in terms of your involvement, and perhaps they will want to keep you on as advisor.

The following are some positive reasons to choose this exit strategy:

- You can sell your business to someone who has experience in the company and who you know and trust.
- As you're still selling the business, you should be able to make some money off the deal.
- If you want to remain involved in some capacity, the management or employees who are buying your business should be more likely to keep you on.
- Your business legacy will remain somewhat intact.

The following are some negative reasons not to choose this exit strategy:

- You may not be able to find a manager or employee who wants to buy the business from you.
- You may find that these management changes are difficult to implement and may have a negative effect on existing clients.
- **Sell to Employees**: You can sell your company to your employees. One common method for funding a sale of a small business to employees is through an Employee Stock Ownership Plan (ESOP). Rather than selling the business to a single employee, an ESOP enables you to transfer ownership of the business to all qualified employees. ESOPs are usually treated as a workforce benefit whereby employees receive an ownership stake in the business as part of their compensation. When an ESOP is used to fund a sale, the employees invest cash in the ESOP, which is then used to acquire the owner's shares in the business over time.

The following are some positive reasons to choose this exit strategy:

- Your employees are already familiar with your business and your customers. If you plan for this exit strategy, you'll have time to acquaint your employees with all aspects of your business.
- This sale will help maintain relationships with customers, vendors, and other employees, and a sense of familiarity in the wake of your absence will keep the transition from causing any drastic changes as you exit.
- Selling to employees ensures a much shorter sale process, which means a more clean-cut break for you.

The following are some negative reasons not to choose this exit strategy:

- If your employees have never had experience running a small business, learning the obligations of ownership could be difficult and lead to failure.
- You could feel obligated to stick around and try to help when you really just want to leave and retire.
- **Sell to the Public**: Many entrepreneurs dream of one day selling their business to the public via an initial public offering (IPO) for a large profit. However, in the realm of small business exit strategy planning, this method certainly isn't for everyone. Business conditions need to be just right for this option to be possible. Even if your business is booming, your industry may not appeal to the public in a way that gets stock buyers excited, thus devaluing your company. This being said, however, if it's possible for you and the conditions are right, an IPO can be very lucrative.

The following are some positive reasons to choose this exit strategy:

- Of all the business exit strategies out there, this is probably the one that's most likely to earn you a substantial profit.
- Your legacy is preserved and can become a household name.

The following are some negative reasons not to choose this exit strategy:

- This is probably one of the most difficult exit strategies, requiring certain conditions and significant time, effort, and money.
- Going public also means intense scrutiny from shareholders and analysts as well as a number of requirements that must be met and processes that must be completed.
- IPO success is very difficult and rare, especially for many small to medium-sized businesses.

A planned exit strategy will help reduce owner dependency and perhaps further empower a management team that can either take over ownership or help a new owner continue to run the company successfully. Where do you envisage being when it comes to small business exit strategy planning? Although much of what's ultimately involved with your exit strategy will be unique to your business, there are a few questions you can ask yourself to get started in your exit plan.

Do You Want to Stay Involved in the Business?

When you are just starting your business, this question might seem almost counterintuitive. Yet, even at an early stage in your endeavor, it's important to be realistic and this means thinking far into the future and considering your business exit strategy. Even if you spend your entire career owning the same business, most people eventually plan to retire at a certain age. Have you set up your business to accomplish that possibility down the line? Maybe you know that you can only withstand business ownership for up to 10 years. What would you ideally like to happen at that point? Would you still want to be involved in the business even if you weren't the owner?

What Are Your Financial Goals?

This is different for everyone. As you are planning for your exit, there are aspects to consider. Will the sale price of your business be enough money for you to retire or seek other endeavors? Can you create a revenue stream of income as an advisor to the new owner? Whatever your goals may be, this question will greatly play into your exit strategy outcome.

If you are aware of the factors that indicate whether selling your business is a good idea, you can time the sale to take advantage of high prices. Usually, you will get the most for your company when your internal sales are climbing and profits are strong. If you have a history of solid performances, by all means sell the company before trouble strikes. Other factors that may affect the timing of a sale are availability of bank financing, interest rate trends, changes in tax law, and the general economic climate.

You can sell your business yourself, but many business owners hire a business attorney, a certified public accountant (CPA), and a professional business broker to handle the transaction. Your business attorney will advise you on the relevant legal and preparation considerations; your CPA will advise you on the tax ramifications; and your business broker protects your anonymity and confidentiality as he or she seeks buyers for your company. If you are advertising your business for sale and showing it to prospects, it could compromise your ability to continue leading the company. Your business broker can be the face for your business, screening prospects and keeping the identity of your business secret from all but qualified buyers.

Selling your business may be preferable to owning if:

- You are ready to retire and have no heirs to continue the company.
- Partners who own the business decide to dissolve their partnership.
- One of the owners dies or becomes disabled and is unable to participate in the business.
- You or another owner get divorced and need cash for a settlement.

- You want to do something more challenging, more fun, and less stressful.
- You do not have enough working capital to keep the business going.
- The company needs new skills, a new approach, or resources you cannot provide.

Most business buyers are individuals like you who want to become small business owners. But sometimes you can transfer ownership of your business to another business in a merger or acquisition. As a rule, businesses have deeper pockets and borrowing power than individuals, and they may be willing to pay more than individuals. Businesses also tend to be more savvy buyers than individuals, increasing the chances that your business will survive, albeit perhaps as a division or subsidiary of another company. So, how do you prepare your business for a merger or acquisition?

Merging your business with another business may be preferable if:

- Your company has a strong financial history.
- Your company's technology and intellectual property are protected.
- Customer sales and loyalty are strong.
- Your employees are willing to continue with the new owner.
- Your company is a proper fit for the buyer.

The best candidate for a merger is a company that sees your business as a strategic fit. If you have something it wants, such as a unique product or distribution channel, the purchaser may be willing to pay a premium price.

Sometimes, the best thing to do is simply sell your inventory and fixtures, pay your creditors and employees, close your doors, and walk away.

Closing your company may be the best option if:

- Your business is failing.
- Your business is not valuable enough for anyone to want to acquire it.
- Your business is the type of business that is unlikely to be valuable without you personally operating it.

What Should I Know Before Exiting My Business?

Selling your business is never an easy or simple process. It is exactly that: a process. Ideally, an exit strategy is planned at the outset of a business. However, because businesses are so fluid, it can be difficult to know what the final version of the business will look like. For a mature company, the sooner a plan is put into place, the better prepared an owner will be when an exit is available, both personally and professionally.

The planning starts with determining your personal and business goals, and then assessing your mental and financial readiness. After that you need to identify the exit options most aligned with your goals. When helping clients prepare for their exit, I have found that having discussions on six key factors tend to maximize their chances of success:

1. **Potential Does Not Sell**: Sometimes business owners believe they have a potential gold mine and expect a high selling price based on perceived potential alone. This is not how it works. Buyers want to acquire something that is already successful and a proven business.

2. **Buyers Are Interested in Profits, Not Revenue**: Revenue sounds good. But when it comes down to it, the only number that matters is the profit margin your business makes. Revenue can be cash coming into your business but after expenses and everything else is deducted, what are you left with? The bottom line that potential buyers want to see is the profit margin.

3. **Honest Financials**: The only documents that all buyers look at are the business financials and verifiable proof of those financials, such as invoices and bank deposits reflecting your numbers. Financials should be prepared by your CPA and reflect the true condition of your business.

4. **Past Successes Are Not Recent Successes**: The previous success of a business is largely irrelevant at the time of sale, especially if your business has been struggling toward the end. Buyers are interested in recent performance, usually the last 12 months, and future sustainability. Buyers are not interested in fixing and recovering your business (unless it's Marcus Lemonis, the star of the tv show *The Profit*), especially if you are expecting them to pay a premium. However, make sure you show the buyer previous years if the business has been growing steadily. Buyers love to see growing revenue and profit figures, especially if you have already made future plans for the business that seem realistic based on past performance.

5. **Honesty Is the Best Policy**: The truth is always going to surface, so be up-front about everything from the beginning. Experienced buyers understand that every business has positives and negatives. There is no such thing as a perfect business. If you are honest and transparent from the start, there is less risk of a deal going sour because the buyer uncovered something during due diligence that wasn't presented accurately. Honesty is the best policy in all business transactions, and selling your business is no different.

6. **Expect to Answer Questions**: I'm sure you would not walk into a house and decide to buy it without first asking a lot of questions. The same

is true of your business. Prospects will not buy a business without first asking a lot of questions, and you need to be prepared to answer them, regardless of how simple or complex they may be. Never judge buyers; you never know who you are dealing with or the buying power they possess.

When Should I Exit My Business?

Another very important factor that you should know before selling your business is when to sell your business. Timing is everything, and crucial in the process of exiting your business. There are circumstances where bad timing is not a huge deal, but choosing the wrong time to sell your business can be the difference between realizing the optimal deal or leaving money on the table. When to sell your business is just as important as how to sell your business and only by knowing both can you confidently pursue the maximum value. History has shown us that there are two conditions that indicate it's an ideal time to sell:

- When your business is doing well and making money; and
- When buyers are active

You should be aware at all times of your annual financials, the position of your business, and whether the direction is positive. It's important not to fall into the trap of waiting for your business to suffer to consider selling. Buyers are most active during a seller's market. This is when the economy is strong and the demand for businesses among buyers is greater than the supply of businesses, raising the value of companies. Typical conditions of a seller's market include:

- Positive economic environment
- Low or modest interest rates
- Low capital gains taxes
- High cash balances
- Strong earnings

To give yourself the best chance of exiting for the maximum value, understanding the signs of a seller's market means you can tell when the conditions are right to sell your business.

Key Takeaways

- Deciding to leave or sell the business you have worked so hard to grow is rarely an easy decision. As you think about your business exit strategy, you'll not only want to consider how you'll leave, but other factors that are involved with this process. Will you make money when you exit your business? What will happen to your business after you leave? How long will your exit take? Understanding your options could be the difference between selling at a premium or leaving money on the table.
- Selling your business is never an easy or simple process. It is exactly that: a process. Ideally, an exit strategy is planned at the outset of a business. However, because businesses are so fluid, it can be difficult to know what the final version of the business will look like. For a mature company, the sooner a plan is put into place, the better prepared an owner will be when an exit is available, both personally and professionally.
- Another very important factor that you should know before selling your business is when to sell your business. Timing is everything and crucial in the process of exiting your business.

CHAPTER 11

How Do I Prepare for Exit?

Every small business owner pours more than long hours into their company to make it a success. We all know that there are plenty of tears, sacrifices, and struggles to make a small business stand on its own two feet, which makes the decision to sell all the more complicated. When my clients get to this stage and are ready for sale, the number two question most frequently asked in the Exit phase is how to prepare for exit.

How Do I Prepare for Exit?

To answer this question, you need to consider the reason for the sale so you can explain it to buyers. This is one of the first questions a potential buyer will ask: "Why are you selling?" In my experience, business owners commonly sell their company for any of the following reasons:

- Retirement
- Partnership disputes
- Illness and death
- Being overworked
- Boredom
- Not making money

Selling a small business can be a complicated process, both emotionally and logistically, and requires careful planning. You'll have to get your company in tip-top shape before entertaining serious offers, and make sure your financials are rock solid at all times. Here is a checklist I have created for my clients who want to get their business ready for sale, which I call the 6 Bs of preparation:

1. **Business Financials**: Financial statements are written records of your business's financial situation. They include standard reports, such as balance sheets, profit and loss statements, and cash flow statements. Selling a business means that you're going to have a lot of eyes on your financials; this includes accountants, lawyers, business brokers, business valuations specialists, and your prospective buyers and their team of professionals. Work with your accountant to make sure your financial information is in great shape. You'll need to provide, on average, three years' worth of tax returns and financial statements as part of your sale. Also, be ready to account for all company income during this period, as any missing money sends a red flag to prospective buyers. Remember, serious buyers are business savvy and don't like to see surprises, which could kill the deal before it's begun. Be prepared to share your year-to-date financials when selling your business, as buyers want to know that they are investing in a thriving company rather than one in financial turmoil.

2. **Business Valuation**: The value of any business is what a willing and informed buyer will pay for it. Of course, the process of determining a company's value is a bit more complex than that. When selling your business, you can generally expect to price your company anywhere from three to six times your current cash flow. This is a helpful place to start but there's a massive difference between the low and high ends of this range. Especially when you factor in other considerations, such as the market for similar sales and overall industry projections. It is always a great idea to bring in a third-party business valuator who can help you get a more precise figure of what your company is really worth. A valuator will determine the actual value of your company based on sales, revenue, outstanding invoices, inventory, and debts. Most of the time, a company is valued on its "EBITDA," which refers to Earnings Before Interest, Taxes, Depreciation, and Amortization. EBITDA is a value that most buyers, investors, and analysts will look to find when deciding which selling business is preferable, as it is a strong indicator of its growth potential.

3. **Business Contracts**: There are a host of legal considerations when selling a business. A thorough due diligence will need to be conducted, especially on existing contracts with clients, vendors, and any other parties you are doing business with. These contracts should contain assignable language, whereby you are allowed to assign your contract under a merger or acquisition of your company. If permission is needed to assign a particular contract to the new owner, then working on getting the approval

letters signed will be an endeavor that will need to be completed before you seek buyers. These contracts become a part of your business assets and having the legal right to sell them along with your other assets only adds to the value of your business. Among those necessary to close the deal is another important contract, the asset purchase agreement, which is a legal contract for the sale and the purchase of your business assets, including physical as well as intellectual property. This comprehensive document will consist of exhibits, including noncompete agreements, asset listings, employee agreements, vendor agreements, and the transfer of any names belonging to the company.

4. **Business Operating Procedures**: If you do not have a written set of detailed standard operating procedures, you need to develop them right away. Build your business operating procedures to the point where, if you get hit by a bus tomorrow, your business will move forward without any disruption. You should detail everything in your standard procedures, including but not limited to executive strategy, including the vision, mission, core values, and management practices; marketing plan, including the tools used to attract prospects to your company; sales plan and procedures, including what tools and processes your business uses to convert prospects to customers; and operating procedures, including detailed processes of how your business works day in and day out.

5. **Business as Usual**: When preparing their business for sale, most entrepreneurs mentally check out and start to relax their approach on how they do business, or don't continue to invest in marketing, which leads to new business. This practice is not condoned in the business world as it ends up hurting the bottom line, your profits, and can be seen as doing harm to your business by not keeping up with your best practices. Having a business that has shown good growth patterns is what you are aiming for all the way up to the time you sell your business, and it's what buyers will want to see. Steady and predictable financial growth is the goal. You may have some dips in your growth patterns here and there, but as long as they can be explained, you will be fine. What a buyer does not want to see is erratic swings in your growth. Making your assets look as good as possible before a sale can help increase your asking price. If you're able to show that your sales are trending upward as you prepare to exit, you'll signal to potential buyers that your company is in great financial shape with plenty of room to grow.

6. **Buyers**: Not every offer to buy your business is going to be made in good faith. Selling a business requires owners to provide tons of sensitive financial and proprietary information. These details are worth a fortune to your competitors and can help them get better insights into your company.

One way to safeguard your sensitive information is to use a nondisclosure agreement (NDA). NDAs prevent buyers and sellers from using sensitive information to undermine one another, and forbid the transmission of information to other parties for as long as the NDA is in place.

What Documents Are Needed to Sell My Business?

There are numerous documents that are crucial in the process of exiting your company. Without these, your business is not protected and it becomes far more difficult to attract buyers to your company, as buyers do not want to walk into potential legal pitfalls. Here is a breakdown of the documents that are needed to sell your business and what information they should include:

- **Offering Memorandum**: Your offering memorandum is a legal document presenting the features of your business that will attract buyers. This is arguably the most important document when selling your business, as it will present detailed information about your company that buyers will want to see before they consider making an offer. The offering memorandum will contain the following information:
  - Three years of historical financials
  - Five years of projected financials
  - Full description of your company, which should include a complete history of the business, its current operations, and future growth opportunities
  - SWOT analysis
  - Analysis of the projected growth of your industry
  - Examination of key clients
  - Disclosure of significant contractual relationships with customers and strategic partners
  - Organizational chart showing critical employees and their relationship with the company
  - Full list of assets, both tangible and intangible, that make the company unique and successful

     It is crucial that your offering memorandum is accurate, as this is what buyers will refer to when conducting due diligence. While it is tempting to hide any negative information in the hope that this increases your sale price, professional buyers will always spot any subversions, which could result in a severe loss of trust.
- **Confidentiality Agreement**: Before sending your offering memorandum to prospective buyers, it is imperative to have a signed confidentiality

agreement with the buyer in question. As your offering memorandum will contain a great deal of sensitive information about your company's financials, customers, employees, and more, this legally binding contract protects you from any of this information being leaked out or used against you.

- **Letter of Intent**: The letter of intent sets the conditions for due diligence to be conducted between those buying and you. This document sets expectations around your deal structure, scheduling, and other big picture aspects of your negotiations, which helps resolve any potential difficulties immediately. It is essentially an agreement for a future agreement. Letters of intent can also act as a means to protect both buyers and sellers. For buyers, they can include a "no-shop" clause that prevents the seller from conducting negotiations with other buyers or continuing to market their business while due diligence is completed. For sellers, a breakup fee can be arranged to help prevent buyers cancelling negotiations for any unpermitted reason, ensuring any loss in time, money, and effort is compensated.

- **Purchase Agreement**: The final agreement that should be drafted to help sell your company is a definitive purchase agreement, which is a legal document that records the conditions for the sale and purchase of a business. This includes all terms and conditions for the acquisition, including form of payment, deal structure, and termination clauses.

How Long Does It Take to Sell My Business?

While every process is unique, in my experience of working with clients during their exit, on average it takes around 15 to 18 months to prepare your business for the sale process. I have had clients lose big offers from buyers because the client was not ready and the buyer was not prepared to wait for nearly two years, which is why it's crucial to begin your preparations as early as possible. You can take steps to ensure your company is as "buyer ready" as possible before beginning the sales process. By taking time to analyze any risks that might impede selling your company, you will reduce the time needed to identify and address any problems at a later stage.

Key Takeaways

- Selling a small business can be a complicated process, both emotionally and logistically, and requires careful planning. You'll have to get your company in tip-top shape before entertaining serious offers, and make sure your financials are rock solid at all times. I presented a checklist of the 6 Bs of preparation.

- There are numerous documents that are crucial in the process of exiting your company. Without these, your business is not protected and it becomes far more difficult to attract buyers to your company as buyers do not want to walk into potential legal pitfalls.
- While every process is unique, in my experience of working with clients during their exit, on average it takes around 15 to 18 months to prepare your business for the sale process.

CHAPTER 12

What Could Go Wrong?

Business owners who are not knowledgeable about their Business Legal Lifecycle® make drastic mistakes when selling their business and lose thousands of dollars in the process. Failure to prepare properly before selling your business and neglecting to closely manage the sales process itself can result in a disappointing outcome. So, what could go wrong? You may not find a buyer, you may fail to achieve the price you want for your business, or the sale may fall through in the later stages of the deal because of due diligence issues or other disruptive events.

The third most frequently asked question in the Exit phase is whether something could go wrong.

What Could Go Wrong?

Whatever the exit strategy, laying the groundwork for a successful sale is one of the most significant challenges a business owner will face. The wrong approach can create major financial consequences. It pays to know your options and which of them is the right fit for your business. Unfortunately, many owners lack the expertise and guidance to identify the proper path to exit and effectively manage key challenges along the way. Here are some of the most common mistakes business owners make while selling their business:

- **Insufficient Preparation**: When preparing your business for sale, take a look at all the things that need to be fixed, such as:
  - Excessive tax deductions should be identified, including running too many discretionary personal expenses through your company. Even if the deductions are legitimate, they lower the earnings of your business and require explanation.

131

- Organize your books and records and make it as simple as possible for the potential buyer to conduct their due diligence. The buyer's legal and financial advisors will want to review all your contracts and governance records, such as minutes of the meetings of the board of directors and shareholders.
- Staffing considerations should be re-evaluated because you should have the right people in the right jobs being paid the right amounts. Once you sell, you would ideally like the staff to continue with the new owner and help run the business.
- Pending or threatening litigation is a huge turn off for potential buyers; you may not be able to resolve everything, although you should take steps to try to resolve the matter. You should disclose any and all matters to the potential buyer and explain how you are handling it, as no buyer wants to walk into a litigation problem right off the bat. This will build credibility and trust between you and the buyer.
- **Mispresenting Company Facts**: As a business owner, it's your responsibility to present your business to the buyer in the best light possible. But never misrepresent your business to a prospective buyer in an attempt to sell it. If you exaggerate numbers before the sale, it can cause you serious trouble once the buyer finds out after the sale. Don't hide any prior investigations or litigation and talk to your advisors as to when to bring up these issues. Get in front of the issues and explain them. Buyers are more empathetic than you think. Your purchase and sale agreement will contain a lot of representations and warranties, such as:
  - The proper formation of your company
  - The capitalization of your company and who owns the company
  - The company has or will pay all taxes due
  - There is no pending or threatened litigation
  - The financial statements and books are accurate
- **Problems with Business Valuation**: Setting a price without undergoing the valuation process can cause your sale to be unfavorable to you. If your price is too low, potential buyers might think that there's something wrong with the business. Setting an extremely high price is obviously going to repel buyers. For a smooth sale, it's a good idea to conduct a thoughtful valuation of your business before putting it on the market.
- **Not Considering the Type of Sale**: Many owners are excited to get an offer to sell their business. They don't spend a lot of time thinking about how to structure the sale. There are two basic ways to sell your business: selling the assets or selling the stock. Asset sales tend to be good for buyers, whereas stock sales favor sellers. The reason sellers prefer stock sales is because the

liabilities of the business usually go along with the stock, but buyers can choose not to assume liabilities in an asset sale.

- **Rushing the Sale**: When a business owner decides to sell, they want the process finished quickly. However, there is a systematic process of identifying prospective buyers, leveraging buyers to induce multiple offers, negotiating the best deal, drafting critical documents, and finally formalizing and signing closing documents. The entire process generally takes between 8 to 12 months and it can be time consuming and cumbersome. It is important to find an intermediary that meticulously manages every step of the selling process on your behalf while you continue to do what you do best, which is run your business.

- **Selling at the Wrong Time**: Many business owners wait too long to sell because they wait too long to begin planning an exit strategy. Waiting too long, or not planning in advance, can cause many business owners to miss their window of opportunity. They invest their entire working life into building a business, which often represents a significant percentage of their retirement fund, only to lose leverage by waiting too long to sell. Long-term planning is key to any successful business sale. With a professional exit plan mapped out, the implementation is executed at exactly the right moment. To limit exposure, and often unforeseen pitfalls such as health issues, downward business turns, burnout, or the desire to pursue other interests, it's important to have a plan in place that you review at least once a year and update as needed.

- **Selling to the Wrong Buyer**: Taking the first offer may not be a wise choice, as this may not necessarily be your best offer. When looking for a buyer for your business, you must know what to look for. Are you willing to sell your business to anyone who offers you the right price? More than likely you have been instrumental in the success and longevity of your business. Surely, you don't want your company to end up in the hands of an owner who does not know what to do with your business. It is essential to find a buyer who has the expertise and experience to run your company effectively. Well-thought-out prequalification criteria can help you access the buyers who are serious about your business. Selecting a qualified buyer who has the necessary experience, management skills, and financial strength to buy your business is vitally important. Don't be shy about conducting a background check on the prospective buyer, as one can tell a lot about a person from what they have done in the past.

When selling a business, usually your advisors will provide you with a checklist that will contain all the necessary steps that need to be taken, along with the assignment of the people who will be responsible for taking those steps. The checklist should include but not be limited to how to best handle the transfer of certain assets, such as:

- Do the business licenses, if any, need to be canceled, or can they be transferred to the new buyer?
- What is going to happen to your trademarks and how do you transfer them to the new buyer?
- Are you responsible for finalizing any outstanding tax obligations?
- Are you able to transfer your lease to your building, or do you need to cancel it by paying early termination fees?
- Are you able to transfer any utility contracts to the new buyer, or do you need to cancel them?

How Do I Minimize Risk When Selling My Business?

As a business owner, you have worked hard all your life to get to the point where you are ready to sell your business and reap the benefits, which can be both overwhelming and emotional. The best strategy is always taking it step by step, allowing yourself to get comfortable with the idea of selling and minimizing the risk of missing important steps. To minimize the risk involved in selling your business, you'll need to plan and prepare well in advance. Here are a few things you can do to minimize your risk while preparing to sell your company:

- **Organize Internal Processes**: You know there are areas where process or key contracts are not as clear as they could be, but the job gets done anyway. A careful review of key business processes, assets, and contracts can save you major hassles during the selling period and significantly increase the value of your business. Some of the areas that often need the most attention include:
  - **Financial Records and Reports**: Ask yourself: Are your financial statements ready for due diligence? Do they reflect the latest GAAP (Generally Accepted Accounting Principles) accounting methods? Have they been reviewed or audited by a respected CPA firm?
  - **Employment Contracts**: Ask yourself: Will your key executives stay once they find out the business is being sold? What will keep them from leaving or competing with your business? Will they have incentive to stick around and help the business be successful after the sale?
  - **Intellectual Property**: Ask yourself: Have you had your business contracts relating to your company's intellectual property reviewed by an intellectual property attorney? Is it clear who owns what? When ownership is not clear, the value of your business can be diminished.

- **Business Legal Structure**: Ask yourself: Is the current legal structure in which the business is owned the most efficient structure for a sale? Will you pay more tax than necessary? Cleaning up the structure before the deal can simplify the transaction and avoid problems when the business is sold, and can potentially save you money on taxes.
- **Assemble the Right Team**: Business owners sometimes avoid seeking help from outside advisors to avoid the fees. Granted, there are a lot of things that business owners can do but experience shows that business owners enjoy much higher net proceeds and far more peace of mind by engaging good advisors. After completing complex negotiations, many business owners recognize that they are their worst when negotiating on their own behalf. Recognize that fact up front and take advantage of the benefits of having highly skilled advisors represent your interests. Once you have your team in place, let them do their job. Some business owners make the mistake of taking over the selling process. Selling a business is a big deal, and it can be emotionally challenging to let go. However, maximizing the sale price for your business requires precisely that, the ability to be objective and detached, which can make all the difference in the outcome. A good team of advisors will listen to you, advise you on your options, help you create a solid strategy, and persuasively advocate for your best interest in the negotiation process.
- **Stay Focused on Your Business:** We have all heard stories about how buyers came back to the table right before the deal was expected to be signed to ask for concessions because the financial results for the months just prior to closing didn't meet expectations. Often the primary cause is that your or your management team's focus was on the deal instead of on your business. Many business owners seem to check out mentally once they plan on exiting their business. This is one of the worst things you can do for your business, your employees, and your customers. This attitude will result in revenue slump because you took your foot off the gas and the business will start showing signs of less profit. When potential buyers find a downward trend in revenue, they will be much less open to paying the asking price. You should continue working on your business as if there is no sale on the horizon. In your exit plan establish clear assignments on who is managing the business and who is working on the exit deal. Do not let the exit process distract you from your most important job, which is conducting business as usual and hitting or exceeding your financial projections. This is another advantage of using outside advisors. Your management team may be aces at growing and operating your business, but they may not be skilled at selling the business.
- **Transition Issues**: Ownership transition can be difficult. Many business owners are so focused on selling their business that they completely neglect

the transition process that will occur after closing. The new owner will need to understand how and why you operated the business the way you did and the reasons behind your decisions. This is not to say the new owner will make the same decisions, but if they can understand the reasons behind previous decisions and make any changes carefully and with consideration, it will increase their chances of success. Some buyers will insist that you remain on for a few months to assist with the transition or training, while others prefer a clean break. Either way is fine, as long as the buyer and you have discussed the transition and reached a mutually acceptable arrangement during negotiations. Another critical piece in the transaction is your customer relationships.

Running a successful business is a challenging yet rewarding adventure. Deciding to end that journey by selling your business can be a tough choice. The process of selling a business is exhausting and difficult, but when it's all said and done, you'll be able to exit your business on your own terms. I have included an Exit Strategy Checklist below that will help you get your legal ducks in a row.

EXIT STRATEGY CHECKLIST

As a business owner, you know that every major decision requires careful thought and preparation; and what bigger decision is there than deciding to sell your business? To sell your business is not as simple as putting up a "for sale" sign. There are lots of things you need to take into consideration and take many steps to prepare. Making these strategic decisions will help you achieve the highest possible valuation of your company.

Here are some action steps you can take when planning the sale of your business:

A. *Make Yourself Redundant*

You are selling your business, not yourself. Buyers will want to see a strong supporting management team. This indicates the business will continue to be successful long after you are out of the picture.

B. *Prepare Early*

You need to start thinking about ways to maximize profitability before deciding to sell your business. Ideally you want to have demonstrable higher earnings when it's time to sell. Focus on achieving those operational efficiencies, cost reductions, and other value enhancers in advance.

C. *Have Strong Financial Controls and Processes*

Having a competent chief financial officer in place is a good start to implementing strong financial controls. Take time to really understand your business operations and look at profitability from an objective standpoint. Never take your eye off the money.

D. *Offer a Realistic and Supportable Forecast*

To most buyers, you are selling the future and future cash flows. Have a realistic and supportable forecast. This points to the credibility of management and the quality of the business. Providing potential buyers with forecasts that are reasonable, believable, and achievable can further demonstrate the underlying value of your business.

E. *Working Capital: Understand It, Manage It, Reduce It*

Working capital is often an overlooked source of value, but it can be difficult for an owner to firmly grasp. Working capital is the lifeblood of a business, and buyers expect to receive a normal level. Managing working capital requires both effort and time, but it can free up trapped cash and can lower the total level of working capital buyers expect to be delivered.

F. *Seek Professional Advice*

Ensure that you have the right team of professionals helping you with accounting, tax, and legal. Each will have their role in the sales process and can provide you with different perspectives and expertise in their respective areas.

What Is Due Diligence?

I have used the word due diligence throughout this book. Let me take a moment to explain what that is and how it should be conducted. Professionals define due diligence as an investigation or audit of a potential investment consummated by a prospective buyer. The objective is to confirm the accuracy of the seller's information and appraise its value. Incomplete or improper investigation is actually one of the major culprits attributed toward the failure of a sale. Therefore, it is critical for sellers to offer accurate information and for buyers to closely investigate potential business sales and understand the true value of the business. Otherwise, both the seller and the buyer could waste a great deal of their valuable time in trying to complete a sales transaction that is doomed from the beginning.

The due diligence process should be all-encompassing, which makes it difficult to even know where to begin or what to look at. When conducting due diligence for my clients, I follow the seven types of investigations that should be undertaken to ensure comprehensive coverage of risk:

1. **Legal**: Legal due diligence helps determine whether the selling company is legally involved with issues. Items assessed include:
   - Contracts
   - Corporate documents
   - Board meeting minutes
   - Corporate compliance
2. **Financial**: Financial due diligence is one of the most critical investigations, as the financials of any business are the true telltale sign of where the business stands at any given time. Items assessed include:
   - Financial statements
   - The company's forecasts and projections
   - Inventory schedules
3. **Human Resources**: Human resources due diligence focuses on the company's most vital asset, their employees. Items assessed include:
   - The company's organizational structure
   - Contracts
   - Compensation and benefits
   - Vacancies
   - Any type of harassment disputes or wrongful terminations
4. **Business**: Business due diligence identifies who the company's customers are and pinpoints its industry. It helps forecast the impact and associated risks that the sale may pose on the buyer's current customers.
5. **Operational**: Operational due diligence involves an examination of all the elements of a company's operations. The object is to evaluate the condition of assets, technology, and facilities and discover any hidden risks or liabilities.
6. **Environmental**: Environmental due diligence verifies that the company's processes, equipment, and facilities are in compliance with environmental regulations. The purpose is to negate the possibility of penalties down the line.
7. **Strategic Fit**: Strategic fit due diligence assesses whether the selling company will be suitable with respect to the buyer's goals and objectives.

Here is a due diligence checklist that you can use to start preparing your business for sale:

DUE DILIGENCE CHECKLIST

A. *Books and Records Up to Date*
   - Review both internal and external documents (i.e., filings with the state and bylaws, minutes, etc.)

- List of owners with their percentage holdings
- List of all states where you do business

B. *Tax and Financial Information*
   - Tax returns and audited financial statements for three years
   - List of all debt
   - List of inventories
   - List of all assets
   - List of accounts receivable and accounts payable
   - Depreciation schedules

C. *Real Estate*
   - List of all real property
   - Copies of all leases

D. *Employees and Benefit Plans*
   - List of employees
   - Copy of Employee Handbook
   - Copies of all qualified employee plans and employee summary plan descriptions
   - Worker's compensation history
   - Unemployment insurance claims history

E. *Licenses and Permits*
   - List of all governmental licenses, permits, or consents
   - Any correspondence or documents relating to any proceedings of any regulatory agency

F. *Environmental Issues*
   - Copies of any Phase I or II audits
   - Copies of any past remedial action
   - Copies of any EPA (Environmental Protection Agency) reports or other orders

G. *Key Products*
   - A list of all key products

H. *Key Relationships and Contracts*
   - List of key customers
   - List of supply or service agreements
   - List of other key contracts

I. *Litigation*
   - List of all pending and contingent litigation

J. *Insurance Coverage*
   - List of all liability, key man, fire, etc. insurance policies
   - List of all covered and uncovered claims for past three years

Key Takeaways

- Whatever the exit strategy, laying the groundwork for a successful sale is one of the most significant challenges a business owner will face. The wrong approach can create major financial consequences. It pays to know your options and which of them is the right fit for your business. Unfortunately, many owners lack the expertise and guidance to identify the proper path to exit and effectively manage key challenges along the way.
- As a business owner, you know that every major decision requires careful thought and preparation; and what bigger decision is there than deciding to sell your business? To sell your business is not as simple as putting up a "for sale" sign. There are lots of things you need to take into consideration and take many steps to prepare. Making these strategic decisions will help you achieve the highest possible valuation of your company.
- The due diligence process should be all-encompassing, which makes it difficult to even know where to begin or what to look at. When conducting due diligence for my clients, I follow the seven types of investigations that should be undertaken to ensure comprehensive coverage of risk.

A STORY OF CAUTION FOR EXITING COMPANIES

How Not to Sell

If I have learned anything from my successful clients, it's this – prepare, prepare, and then prepare, for whatever you decide to do in business. Never enter into anything business related without preparing. Here is a story of caution that happened to a client who wanted to sell her business.

I used to attend a meeting with this one particular client every year, and each time I would ask her, "Bella, have you told your employees that you want them to buy your business?" She had a plan to eventually sell her dog pampering business to her senior employees, but she had yet to inform them of this fact. "I'm not ready yet," she would say.

Then another year passed by and the same thing would happen again: "I'm not ready yet." Finally, she called one day and said, "I'm finally done and want to be out of here in six months."

"Bella," I asked, "have you talked to your employees yet?"

"No," she said.

After some nudging, Bella finally approached the two employees, who had been with her for 12 years. She told them, "I would like to retire in six months, and I'm willing to sell the business to you." Their immediate reaction? They thought the business was in trouble and that Bella was trying to push all the liabilities on to them. The sudden news of the sale was not received well. The two employees felt that Bella had betrayed them, especially since they had worked for her for 12 years. As it happens, the two employees always wanted to buy Bella's company but did not have the money to do so. Six months was not enough time for them to get the financial resources ready and Bella could not find another buyer in time.

After 12 years of hard work, Bella had to close her doors and walk away from what could have been a lucrative payout. Instead, the business she built, her legacy, her retirement, all disappeared because Bella did not prepare for the sale.

Now, this is how Bella's story should have worked out.

I had another client, a general contractor. He was a self-made man and worked hard to create a great reputation for his business within his community. He always knew that he wanted to work until his wife retired from her job and then sell his business to his two employees who had been with him for 15 years.

He told his employees that he was going to retire in five years and wanted to make sure they had the first right of refusal to buy his company. The two employees were thrilled at this opportunity and jumped at the chance. With plenty of time to transition the business over to the employees, my client started to share the internal operations of the business with the employees and started teaching them management skills, skills to interact with clients, and sales skills.

(Continued)

As time went by, the two employees became more and more comfortable with the transition. They started early on exploring their financial options, and allowed my client to become less and less involved in the day-to-day running of the business.

In this story, my client did it right. He gave plenty of notice to his employees, he trained them and integrated them into the business, and did everything right to ensure the success of the business continued without him. My client received the purchase price he wanted and became an advisor to the company, which allowed him to earn money in his retirement. The company is still thriving today and the employees continue to carry on my client's legacy in the community.

If you're going to exit the business you have had for a long time, you should exit the right way by selling it to a buyer you feel comfortable with and selling it for your asking price. This always creates a win-win situation.

Conclusion

Every business has a Business Legal Lifecycle®: a Startup phase, a Growth phase, an Established phase, and an Exit phase. You, as a business owner, have the capacity to become successful by knowing what phase your business is in and how to better prepare to avoid mistakes and pitfalls. Just like playing chess, think ahead and prepare by planning accordingly in each phase. After working with hundreds of business owners, I discovered that the successful ones share some common traits:

- They know where they are in their Business Legal Lifecycle® and have taken appropriate steps to protect their business.
- They create a business strategy and follow it. They make adjustments to the business plan as and when needed to stay on track.
- They follow a financial road map and know at all times what their financial capacity is.
- They create business processes and understand the need to continuously improve them to become more efficient and productive.
- They employ a team of advisors because they don't know what they don't know.
- They are always ready to sell, if and when the time is right.

I hope this book was educational and inspirational. I applaud you, business owners who wake up every day and work hard to do what you love. As an attorney and business owner, I, too, know the pain of hard work, as well as the joy of great rewards.

Here's to you – my fellow business owners!

Go Legal Yourself® Products

What is the number one common mistake that startups and fast-growing companies make during the early stages of their Business Legal Lifecycle®? Not having the RIGHT contracts, which are specialized to accommodate the current phase of their Business Legal Lifecycle®.

Why do you think this is? Simply put, they don't know what they don't know. No one has offered them the complete specialized legal package relevant to where they are in their business, plus a one-stop shop that includes access to an expert in the Business Legal Lifecycle®, until now.

Go Legal Yourself® offers two packages: the **Startup Essentials Package** and the **Growth Essentials Package**. Finally! Specialized packages that include everything a startup company and a company that's growing fast need to legally protect and run a business.

For more information on this packaged please visit: GoLegalYourself.com

Here is a description of what is included in the two legal packages:

Startup Essentials Package:

- Corporation Formation Package
  - Articles of Incorporation
  - Bylaws
  - Sole Incorporator Resolution
  - Organizational Meeting Minutes
  - Founder's Stock Purchase Agreement
  - Subscription Agreement
  - Form SS-4 to obtain Employer Identification Number (EIN) with instructions
  - Form 2553 to file as an S Corporation election with instructions

- Promissory Note
- Client Agreement
- Independent Contractor Agreement
- Website Terms of Use
- Website Privacy Policy
- Website Disclaimer
- One Hour Legal Strategy Session with an attorney

Growth Essentials Package:

- Employee Handbook
- Employee Application Form
- Employee Agreement
- Invention Assignment Agreement
- Nondisclosure Agreement
- Shareholder Resolution Authorizing Stock
- Board of Director Resolution Authorizing Stock
- Director Agreement
- Shareholder Agreement
- Stock Option Plan
- Stock Option Agreement
- Capital-Raising Business Plan Template
- Trademark Logo Assistance – Half Hour
- Three Hours Legal Strategy Session with an attorney

To learn more about these two packages please visit GoLegalYourself.com

About the Website

Thank you for purchasing this book.

You may access the following additional complementary resources provided for your use by visiting: www.wiley.com/go/bagla/golegalyourself.

(Password: Bagla123).

- Business Plan Template
- Contracts Checklist
- IRS 20 Factor Independent Contractor Checklist
- EDD Independent Contractor Determination Checklist
- Go Legal Yourself® Podcast

Have you always wanted to be more? More in life, more in business, or more generally? We all come from different walks of life and all have different upbringings. If you want more, then you can! You cannot let your upbringing or your disadvantages hold you down. You cannot blame the world for your problems and you cannot let yourself be a victim of your own circumstances.

I have heard too many times that "If I can do it . . . you can do it too." Let me be the first to tell you that this is the biggest bull you will ever hear! If I can do it does not mean that you can do it too. If I can do it means that I wanted it so bad that I worked hard and was self-driven to achieve what I wanted. You can do it too, if you want it so bad and you work hard and stay the course, you can achieve it too.

I'm a go-getter. Always have been. People have asked me time and time again, "Where do you get your drive?" I have always answered, "My parents taught me to believe in me." Dad taught me one thing that has never failed me: "If you want something, you must want it from your heart. Otherwise, don't bother!" I would be remiss if I didn't mention my stubbornness, which I get from my mother.

As a self-made woman, I have learned valuable lessons that have made me the leader I am today. These lessons I learned are worth sharing because I know there are other people out there who can become leaders too, and most of all, want to become leaders. If you have always been told you will never amount to anything and no one believed in you, now is the time to change that. Now is the time to believe in YOU!

My favorite quote is:

"Grab the world by the pearls. It's yours for the taking."

— *Kelly Bagla, Esq.*

This book is your guide to achieve your dreams. It's your time to grab the world by the pearls because it's YOURS for the taking!

Agreement with Respect to *Go Legal Yourself*®

Know Your Business Legal Lifecycle® 2nd Edition

Not another legal disclaimer . . . I know what you're thinking. If I weren't an attorney, I'd be thinking the same. But I do have to cover my bum, so do read this agreement and then enjoy the book.

READ THIS. You should carefully read these terms and conditions before accessing or reading *Go Legal Yourself*®, *Know Your Business Legal Lifecycle*® *2nd Edition*. This is an agreement ("Agreement") between you, the Author, and the Publisher. By accessing or reading *Go Legal Yourself*®, *Know Your Business Legal Lifecycle*® *2nd Edition*, you acknowledge that you have read, understand, and accept the following terms and conditions. If you do not agree and do not want to be bound by such terms and conditions, do not access or review *Go Legal Yourself*®, *Know Your Business Legal Lifecycle*® *2nd Edition*.

1. **License Grant**. Subject to the terms of this Agreement, the Publisher grants to you a nonexclusive, revocable, nontransferable, non-sublicensable license to use *Go Legal Yourself*®, *Know Your Business Legal Lifecycle*® *2nd Edition* solely for your own personal or business purposes.

2. **Restrictions**. Your license for *Go Legal Yourself*®, *Know Your Business Legal Lifecycle*® *2nd Edition* and any text, information, graphics, materials, or documents (collectively defined as "Content and Materials") therein are subject to the following additional restrictions and prohibitions on use: You may not (i) copy, print (except for the express limited purpose permitted by Section 1 above), republish, display, distribute, transmit, sell, rent, lease, loan, or otherwise make available in any form or by any means all or any portion of *Go Legal Yourself*®, *Know Your Business Legal Lifecycle*® *2nd Edition* or any Content and Materials; (ii) use *Go Legal Yourself*®,

149

Know Your Business Legal Lifecycle® 2nd Edition or any materials obtained therefrom to develop, or use as a component of, any information storage and retrieval system, database, information base, or similar resource (in any media now existing or hereafter developed), that is offered for commercial distribution of any kind, including through sale, license, lease, rental, subscription, or any other commercial distribution mechanism; (iii) create compilations or derivative works of any Content and Materials from *Go Legal Yourself®, Know Your Business Legal Lifecycle® 2nd Edition*; (iv) use any Content and Materials from *Go Legal Yourself®, Know Your Business Legal Lifecycle® 2nd Edition* in any manner that may infringe any copyright, intellectual property right, proprietary right, or property right of Author, Publisher, or any third parties; (v) remove, change, or obscure any copyright notice or other proprietary notice or terms of use contained in *Go Legal Yourself®, Know Your Business Legal Lifecycle® 2nd Edition*; (vi) make any portion of *Go Legal Yourself®, Know Your Business Legal Lifecycle® 2nd Edition* available through any timesharing system, service bureau, the internet or any other technology now existing or developed in the future; (vii) use *Go Legal Yourself®, Know Your Business Legal Lifecycle® 2nd Edition* in a manner that violates any state or federal laws; and (viii) export or re-export any portion thereof in violation of the export control laws or regulations of the United States.

3. **Copyright**. The content, organization, graphics, design, compilation, magnetic translation, digital conversion, and other matters related to *Go Legal Yourself®, Know Your Business Legal Lifecycle® 2nd Edition* are protected under applicable copyrights, trademarks, and other proprietary (including but not limited to intellectual property) rights. The copying, redistribution, use, or publication by you of any such matters, except as allowed by Section 1 above, is strictly prohibited. You do not acquire ownership rights to any content, document, or other materials contained in *Go Legal Yourself®, Know Your Business Legal Lifecycle® 2nd Edition*. No claim is made to any government-issued forms, agreements, or other content. The copyright to all of the contents in *Go Legal Yourself®, Know Your Business Legal Lifecycle® 2nd Edition* and the forms, agreements, and checklists is owned by the Author or by third parties from whom the content has been licensed.

4. **Forms, Agreements and Documents**. *Go Legal Yourself®, Know Your Business Legal Lifecycle® 2nd Edition* may contain sample forms, agreements, checklists, business documents and legal documents (collectively, "Documents"). All Documents are provided on a nonexclusive license basis only for your personal one-time use for noncommercial purposes,

without any right to relicense, sublicense, distribute, assign, or transfer such license. Documents are provided without any representations or warranties, express or implied, as to their suitability, legal effect, completeness, currentness, accuracy, and/or appropriateness. THE DOCUMENTS ARE PROVIDED "AS IS," "AS AVAILABLE," AND WITH "ALL FAULTS," AND THE AUTHOR AND THE PUBLISHER DISCLAIM ANY WARRANTIES, INCLUDING BUT NOT LIMITED TO THE WARRANTIES OF MERCHANTABILITY AND FITNESS FOR A PARTICULAR PURPOSE. The Documents may be inappropriate for your particular circumstances. Furthermore, state laws may require different or additional provisions to ensure the desired result. You should consult with legal counsel to determine the appropriate legal or business documents necessary for your particular transactions, as the Documents are only samples and may not be applicable to a particular situation. Some Documents are public domain forms or available from public records, but you should check to see if any newer or updated versions have been issued.

5. **No Legal Advice or Attorney-Client Relationship**. Information contained in or made available from *Go Legal Yourself®, Know Your Business Legal Lifecycle® 2nd Edition* is not intended to and does not constitute legal advice, recommendations, mediation, or counseling under any circumstance, and no attorney–client relationship is formed. No warranty or guarantee is made as to the accurateness, completeness, adequacy, or currentness of the information contained in *Go Legal Yourself®, Know Your Business Legal Lifecycle® 2nd Edition*. Your use and reliance of information in *Go Legal Yourself®, Know Your Business Legal Lifecycle® 2nd Edition* is entirely at your own risk.

6. **Indemnification**. You agree to indemnify, defend, and hold the Author and the Publisher and their partners, agents, officers, directors, employees, subcontractors, successors, assigns, third party suppliers of information and documents, product and service providers, and affiliates (collectively "Affiliated Parties") harmless from any liability, loss, claim, and expense related to your breach of this Agreement.

7. **Disclaimer**. THE INFORMATION, CONTENT AND DOCUMENTS FROM OR THROUGH *GO LEGAL YOURSELf®, KNOW YOUR BUSINESS LEGAL LIFECYCLE® 2ND EDITION* ARE PROVIDED "AS-IS," "AS AVAILABLE," WITH "ALL FAULTS," AND ALL WARRANTIES, EXPRESS OR IMPLIED, ARE DISCLAIMED (INCLUDING BUT NOT LIMITED TO THE DISCLAIMER OF ANY IMPLIED WARRANTIES OF MERCHANTABILITY AND FITNESS FOR A PARTICULAR PURPOSE). *GO LEGAL YOURSELf®, KNOW YOUR BUSINESS LEGAL LIFECYCLE® 2ND*

EDITION MAY CONTAIN ERRORS, PROBLEMS, OR OTHER LIMITATIONS. THE AUTHOR, PUBLISHER, AND THEIR AFFILIATED PARTIES HAVE NO LIABILITY WHATSOEVER FOR YOUR USE OF *GO LEGAL YOURSELf*®, *KNOW YOUR BUSINESS LEGAL LIFECYCLE*® *2ND EDITION*, EXCEPT AS PROVIDED IN SECTION 8(B). IN PARTICULAR, BUT NOT AS A LIMITATION THEREOF, THE AUTHOR, PUBLISHER, AND THEIR AFFILIATED PARTIES ARE NOT LIABLE FOR ANY INDIRECT, SPECIAL, INCIDENTAL, OR CONSEQUENTIAL DAMAGES (INCLUDING, BUT NOT LIMITED TO, DAMAGES FOR LOSS OF BUSINESS, LOSS OF PROFITS, LITIGATION, OR THE LIKE), WHETHER BASED ON BREACH OF CONTRACT, BREACH OF WARRANTY, TORT (INCLUDING NEGLIGENCE), PRODUCT LIABILITY, OR OTHERWISE, EVEN IF ADVISED ON THE POSSIBILITY OF SUCH DAMAGES. THE NEGATION AND LIMITATION OF DAMAGES SET FORTH ABOVE ARE FUNDAMENTAL ELEMENTS OF THE BASIS OF THE BARGAIN BETWEEN AUTHOR, PUBLISHER, AND YOU. *GO LEGAL YOURSELf*®, *KNOW YOUR BUSINESS LEGAL LIFECYCLE*® *2ND EDITION* WOULD NOT BE PROVIDED WITHOUT SUCH LIMITATIONS. NOTHING IN *GO LEGAL YOURSELf*®, *KNOW YOUR BUSINESS LEGAL LIFECYCLE*® *2ND EDITION* SHALL CREATE ANY WARRANTY, REPRESENTATION, OR GUARANTEE NOT EXPRESSLY STATED IN THIS AGREEMENT.

8. **Limitation of Liability**.
   a. The Author, Publisher, and any Affiliated Party shall not be liable for any loss, injury, claim, liability, or damage of any kind resulting in any way from (i) any errors in or omissions from *Go Legal Yourself*®, *Know Your Business Legal Lifecycle*® *2nd Edition*, or (ii) your use of *Go Legal Yourself*®, *Know Your Business Legal Lifecycle*® *2nd Edition*.
   b. THE AGGREGATE LIABILITY OF THE AUTHOR, THE PUBLISHER, AND THE AFFILIATED PARTIES IN CONNECTION WITH ANY CLAIM ARISING OUT OF OR RELATING TO *GO LEGAL YOURSELf*®, *KNOW YOUR BUSINESS LEGAL LIFECYCLE*® *2ND EDITION* SHALL NOT EXCEED THE COST OF *GO LEGAL YOURSELf*®, *KNOW YOUR BUSINESS LEGAL LIFECYCLE*® *2ND EDITION*, AND THAT AMOUNT SHALL BE IN LIEU OF ALL OTHER REMEDIES WHICH YOU MAY HAVE AGAINST THE AUTHOR, THE PUBLISHER, AND ANY AFFILIATED PARTY.

9. **Miscellaneous**. This Agreement shall be treated as though it were executed and performed in San Diego, California, and shall be governed by and construed in accordance with the laws of the State of California (without regard to conflict of law principles). Any cause of action by you with respect to *Go Legal Yourself®, Know Your Business Legal Lifecycle® 2nd Edition* must be instituted within one year after the cause of action arose or be forever waived and barred. All actions shall be subject to the limitations set forth in Section 7 and Section 8. The language in this Agreement shall be interpreted as to its fair meaning and not strictly for or against any party. Any rule of construction to the effect that ambiguities are to be resolved against the drafting party shall not apply in interpreting this Agreement. If any provision of this Agreement is held illegal, invalid, or unenforceable for any reason, that provision shall be enforced to the maximum extent permissible, and the other provisions of this Agreement shall remain in full force and effect. If any provision of this Agreement is held illegal, invalid, or unenforceable, it shall be replaced, to the extent possible, with a legal, valid, and unenforceable provision that is similar in tenor to the illegal, invalid, or enforceable provision as is legally possible. The Author's or the publisher's failure to enforce any provision of this Agreement shall not be deemed a waiver of such provision nor of the right to enforce such provision. The title, headings, and captions of this Agreement are provided for convenience only and shall have no effect on the construction of the terms of this Agreement.

10. **Arbitration**. Any legal controversy or legal claim arising out of or relating to this Agreement and *Go Legal Yourself®, Know Your Business Legal Lifecycle® 2nd Edition* shall be settled solely by confidential binding arbitration in accordance with the commercial arbitration rules of JAMS, before one arbitrator. Any such controversy or claim shall be arbitrated on an individual basis, and shall not be consolidated in any arbitration with any claim or controversy of any other party. The arbitration shall be conducted in San Diego, California. Each party shall bear its own attorneys' fees. Each party shall bear one-half of the arbitration fees and costs incurred through JAMS. The arbitrator shall not have the right to award punitive damages or speculative damages to either party and shall not have the power to amend this Agreement.

DO NOT ACCESS OR READ *GO LEGAL YOURSELf®, KNOW YOUR BUSINESS LEGAL LIFECYCLE® 2ND EDITION* UNLESS YOU UNDERSTAND AND AGREE WITH THE FOREGOING AGREEMENT.

Index